Small Towns, Austere Times

The Dialectics of Deracinated Localism

Small Towns, Austere Times

The Dialectics of Deracinated Localism

Steve Hanson

Winchester, UK
Washington, USA

First published by Zero Books, 2014
Zero Books is an imprint of John Hunt Publishing Ltd., Laurel House, Station Approach,
Alresford, Hants, SO24 9JH, UK
office1@jhpbooks.net
www.johnhuntpublishing.com
www.zero-books.net

For distributor details and how to order please visit the 'Ordering' section on our website.

ISBN: 978 1 78099 998 2

A CIP catalogue record for this book is available from the British Library.

Design: Lee Nash

Printed in the USA by Edwards Brothers Malloy

We operate a distinctive and ethical publishing philosophy in all
areas of our business, from our global network of authors to
production and worldwide distribution.

CONTENTS

Dedication and acknowledgments

This book is dedicated to both my parents. It would not be possible without their generosity in my life, and it is partly about their lives. In this sense, it is also offered to all my friends and relatives in Todmorden, all of whom understand private troubles, with or without their public issues. In particular, I extend this to Roger Birch, whose archive of Todmorden photography I drew on for this work. Sadly, Roger passed away in February 2013.

I also want to thank my PhD supervisor, Les Back, for his enormous kindness and patience, and Robert Galeta and Simon Ford, who showed me the way to go.

INTRODUCTION

I

'Totally Locally', green radicals and the rural right

Picture a valley in northern England with high sides. A river runs through it. It is bleak in winter, but expands like a green lung in summer. A canal, a railway line and a road also run through the valley. They weave around each other, over bridges and under tunnels, which connect the towns along the valley to Leeds in the north and Manchester in the south.

This deep, north-south Pennine gash is dissected from the east and west by the border of two counties, Yorkshire and Lancashire. Right on this crossroads is a town. Its town hall is split in two: a frieze on its neo-classical frontage depicts agricultural work on the Yorkshire side, and cotton production on the Lancashire side. For the size of the place, with 17,000 inhabitants, the town hall is enormous, designed by John Gibson, an assistant to Sir Charles Barry, who designed the Houses of Parliament in London. The public park is also on a London scale. These spaces are reminders that the town was one of the hubs and coils of the industrial machine in the nineteenth-century northwest. The canal and railway were its wiring, connected up to the proto-typical capitalist calculating machine in nearby Manchester.[1]

This is Todmorden. Of course, Todmorden is now a post-industrial town – it calls itself a 'market town', and the population has almost halved since its industrial heyday.

Western imperialism, inseparable from those emerging circuits of capitalism, brought raw materials such as cotton into the town to be processed and exported. The town also saw inward migration, and now around four percent of the population are registered as Muslim. But this word 'inward' is insidious, see how it trips off the tongue. 'Inward' only makes

3

sense if one views 'Old England' as the centre of a new colonial empire, and times have changed: In the 1990s, a Buddhist monastery occupied an old cotton baron's mansion on the moor above the valley here. It had previously been used as a borstal. This said a great deal about the post-industrial afterlife of the town, and the sudden disappearance of the entire organised Buddhist community to Tibet a few years ago now says much about the global network of which this town is just another node.[2]

Yet despite the town's undeniable opening-out to the global, 'localism' is still inherently entwined with forms of inward thinking which can become dangerous, particularly as the eurozone crisis and recession deepens. If we walk up a particular valley side, just below the moorland the valley cuts into, we will find an old ruined farmhouse, which is more eighteenth century than nineteenth, twentieth or twenty-first, with its cracked stone flags, ancient fireplaces and crumbling stone walls. Here lives Michael Smith, who, until very recently, was the 'commissioner' of the Britain For The British Party, a senior, military-style title, within an American-style, neo-Nazi organisation.

Smith looks like a clichéd redneck or hillbilly, with his beard and mid-western American agricultural clothes. But this image slips in the eyes of the public: for some people in the town he looks like a clichéd 'lefty', and a few of them assume that he is actually left-wing. The Britain For The British Party is tiny, but they have a notorious ex-member in Sean Judd, currently serving a sixteen year prison sentence for a range of offences. Five years ago, police raided the truck driver's home in Newcastle, tipped off about child pornography – which they found – along with a Nazi-style flag in a bedroom and the makings of a small holocaust: nail bombs, gunpowder, fuses, bullets, swords, axes, knives, a bayonet and information on how to poison people.

This town is not known for its neo-Nazis, even though it is situated inside a wider web of towns known for race hate, for

4

instance Burnley, Oldham and Rochdale. If this town is now known for anything beyond its borders, it is for its 'green radicals', local growing groups who plant vegetables in the town which anyone can pick, who have an agenda to make the town self-sufficient in food by 2018. This green group successfully projects itself through the circuits of national and international media, yet within the municipal borders, neo-Nazi Michael Smith pulled twenty-one more votes in recent local elections than the Green Party.

Taking his cue from the British National Party, who in recent years have attempted to elide their hard fascist roots, Smith recently tried to make his image more 'friendly'. But this led to him being expelled from his own party, as the makeover involved bringing a female, east Asian Fascist to the town for a few days of canvassing. They chatted to Pakistani market stall-holders, and Smith posted pictures of this day out on his blog. A dictat was then issued by Britain For The British Party central, expelling Smith immediately for 'mingling with the gook public'. Smith also posted photographs of himself with the Asian fascist, posing with rifles and pistols, in front of swastika flags, pictures of Hitler, and reproductions of romantic landscapes in oils. The ancient cracked stone flags and fireplaces of the ruined farmhouse were the default backdrop to these photographs.

This backdrop is not merely incidental detail. During the industrial era, people clung on to the 'old ways', as the industrial revolution irreversibly swept all before it. If we return to E.P. Thompson's 1963 text *The Making of the English Working Class*, we can see how the followers of Joanna Southcott and other apocalyptic religious sects thrived in this area, as enlightenment ways of knowing and doing swept her cult into history.[3] When I see Michael Smith, struggling with his leaflets, and himself, down the street – Smith walks with the exaggerated, aggressive gait of the truly frightened – I see the cult of Southcott. But I recognise the same thing very strongly in my own 'left-wing' perspective on the world as well. In my mind, I have taken the path away from what is and into my own inner landscape, which presents similar dangers, particularly when strong emotional ties with place are at stake.

The concept of 'old' England and newer empires is not buried in dead decades, nor is 'revolution', it invisibly shape shifts to re-inhabit the present, and great care needs to be taken with the mental processes which can be triggered through inherited culture.

Of course, great care also needs to be taken not to confuse older, inactive cults, such as Southcottianism, with the cult of Hitler, in an area noted for its fascist elements. As I write, the Anders Breivik trial in Oslo has just ended. Smith has posted what looks like correspondence between himself and Breivik on his blog, which he has attempted to caveat by arguing against some of Breivik's ideas. It is unclear whether these posts are genuine or not, but the wider point I want to make here is that there is nothing exclusively local about nasty localisms: Michael Smith's attempts to re-localise – mentally – into smaller and smaller borders, this country, this county, this town, and then eventually to his own remote farm, where he is pictured with his hunting rifle and swastika, are actually underpinned by the unfettered global circulation of fascist rhetoric, which is itself hybrid and hybridising. This man accesses his information in the Public Library in the centre of town, provided for by the 'liberals' on the town council whom he despises. Yet the provision of the library is under threat, and the library opening hours have been reduced. This man sits inside one very large signifier of the way that public life is moving, he is literally sitting in the instability, completely oblivious, as he communicates within global flows which never cease, about the need to make things stable, as he sees it, in particular ways. The way he 'sees it' is also being constructed by these flows, he does not simply step into them to make contributions or interventions. There is then, if we understand the processes this way, nothing particularly national about nationalism either.

As we can see, the local neo-Nazi, thrown out of his own party for conspiring with eastern Asian fascists is a story which holds serious contradictions. But those contradictions don't end with Michael Smith. A man I spoke to last week told me that the recession didn't exist, only seconds before he blamed the recession on 'workshy cunts'. This brings me to a big point I want to make here: we can no longer move through these landscapes – practically or intellectually – in a binary way, a dialectical approach is crucial, a dialectics of localism is required, because dialectical thinking can hold and explore inherent contradictions. I will explain this further as we go on.

'Localism' is on one hand perhaps essential, as climate change bites and networks of provision are required to shrink, but how the retrenchment into smaller borders happens sociologically concerns me greatly. 'The local' is the unwritten space of utopia in one sense: the place we have no choice but to go, but of course a lot depends on how that place is written, and it is being written in a bad order in many places, for many different and complex reasons.

Here, it is still essentially being written out of the bitterness of post-industrialism. This is a post-Empire landscape, although not necessarily a post-imperial one. In this sense, the 'utopia' thesis is wrong, there is never a completely blank space to be written. The local growing groups incubate fragments of old Co-operative movements borne out of the need to survive industri-alism, and they also bear traces of apocalyptic old Methodism, at the same time as they distance themselves from the 'new age'. Middle class, former HBOS banking staff are symbolically detox-ifying themselves after the 2008 crash which HBOS contributed to, by moving into localist, organic food production. Here, many people are trying to step into the dark of the oncoming and uncertain landscape, by re-fashioning a new symbolic cloak,

7

which actually fuses older fabrics and decorative figures together in particular ways.

This brings me to the other big question I want to address here, that of provincialism. Like many of the big themes I want to address in this book, provincialism is a mis-understood concept, and the quality literature to be found on the subject is tiny. Provincialism is not 'of' the provinces. It is not essentially geographical, just as there is nothing fundamentally national about nationalism. If accused of provincialism, people are likely to recoil because you are attacking their place of belonging as 'being provincial'. 'How dare you! We are not provincial!' Right at that moment, when they refute the idea that they may be provincial, they are positing a provincial argument: In order to accuse me of accusing their locale of being provincial, they are fencing the accuser off, and right at that moment, by placing the accuser 'outside', they have either become provincial, or revealed their provincialism. Many conversations I overheard or took part in during research took this shape.

Provincialism is also not 'of' the provinces, in the sense that 'provincial' people are often designated as those who use national and nationalistic arguments. Racists such as Michael Smith use all the containers available, he talks of 'true locals' and the 'truly British', in spite of Britain's current status as a very hybrid nation with strongly secessionist elements. His arguments are quite literally all-over-the-place, despite trying to be exclusively of one place, and I want to make a case here for a way of thinking which can somehow deal with that slipperiness.

If people could 'do' localism without excluding the other, without re-locating their own provincialism, racism or elitism in their sense of the 'radical', we could maybe call these processes 'utopian'. But we might instead think of the term 'atopos' here, meaning out of place, or unbecoming. Michael Smith, the neo-Nazi, is an anomaly in many ways, but some of the rather cosy, localist networks are classed in a bad order, they are nostalgic, and they fetishise the rural in a way which resembles the volkisch movements in Germany. In Britain, figures such as William Morris clung to similar ideas. In Germany, 'the local' gradually became an Aryan meeting place where the Jews don't go.

It would be vastly excessive to claim that this is happening here, but it isn't excessive to claim that this is not simply a set of rainbow, 'elective communities', singing and dancing at the end of history. This is history opening again after the amnesia of the bubble years, but the idea that people are now 'waking up' needs to be resisted, until it can be proven that they are not simply falling into other, perhaps older dreams.

2

Several returns

As we walk around this small town, I want to explain some of the philosophical thinking behind my return to it. Todmorden is my 'home town', although that cosy phrase now has little meaning on a rapid, globalised landscape. Taking their cue from C. Wright Mills, both Zygmunt Bauman and Ulrich Beck have asked us to try to seek public solutions to private problems, and this is largely what I am attempting here.[4] I have made several returns to this place over the course of my life, I have not remained here in an unbroken line, nor does anyone else remain neatly in one channel during their lives.

In one sense, there are two forms of time working together as I write: a long immersion in this place; and the shorter time of distilling that into a book. Yet explaining what is happening as I write like this is all too easy and neat. Because immersion in time and place does not necessarily mean knowing. When I was growing up here, I lived in a row of worker cottages from the late eighteenth century. A story existed that John Wesley had written something on the gable end of this row, which had been sealed up by its rendering. But on returning, as a researcher, I find that the dates don't match. Growing up here did not give me a stronger or more privileged access to 'truth', growing up here gave me an increased exposure to myth. So being 'of' a place is doubly impossible, not only is it impossible due to the rapid circulation of value globally, but it is impossible because there is no simple equation to be set up between long exposure to place and wisdom. Of course, some very old people are very wise, but some are not, quite the opposite.

These points may seem anecdotal, but actually, they led me – eventually – to return to dialectical thinking. Because as we can see, just walking around the town, many of the people here display inherent contradictions, and so a philosophical and epistemological approach to landscapes such as these needs to be found, one which can deal with contradiction, and that approach is proper dialectical thinking. Todmorden is a border town, it sits on the border of Lancashire and Yorkshire. This used to be easy to figure out, the county border once ran with the river, underneath the town hall, cutting it in two, giving it a Lancashire side and a Yorkshire side. Now, the geographical border is situated some way out of the town. Todmorden is now 'in' Yorkshire, but has a Lancashire postcode and telephone dial code. The way the local borders have been made fuzzy as the place became modernised speaks to the wider social situation, but it also describes any attempt to go to small towns such as these to research and write about them. The neat, clear borders are of the past for thinking, for epistemology, for the production of knowledge, as much as they are for identity and belonging.

This said, the borders placed around who owns what have not become fuzzy, this, it has to be stated, remains. But what became very clear here was the need for a solution to all the epistemological problems I have begun to outline. Because not only have simple things such as land line dialling codes problematised the idea of 'borders' here, the land lines themselves have become quaint little antiques. We need guidance on how to return to small towns, where various groups stubbornly continue to declare themselves unique and singular, whilst existing in a relativistic universe. We need, in places such as these, a way of working with contradiction.

3

Practical dialectics

This is an argument about the usability of dialectical thinking, now, in 2013. This may sound very 'lofty', but I actually want to return the dialectic to practical use, but for a globalised world, via the concept of the 'trace'. Ultimately, I also want to argue that this is a political act. In 2013, capitalism is still the one remaining Western grand narrative, although its remaining also contains its radical instability. Its inherent contradictions have been migrating to the surface of its discourses since 2008, although this is not the same thing as saying its end is nigh, or that this 'nigh' is inevitable, quite the opposite. Nobody needs to be a philosopher to understand this. Yet Marx's work is flying out of bookshops, and at a conference presentation by Mike Savage recently, we were shown data from a very large class survey, which Marx would have understood well.[5] I want to explore some of the philosophical ramifications of revisiting dialectical thinking now, in a necessarily truncated form.

The first thing we need to do is revisit the dialectic in order to understand it as *'aufheben'*, or 'sublation', and not just as the 'thesis-antithesis-synthesis' process it is often explained to be.

The dialectic is often laid out as a positive colliding with a negative, which then fuse chemically, producing a synthesis. But before we go any further, we need to understand the dialectic as something quite radically other than a simple 'discourse'. For Hegel, *'aufheben'* means processes which are both preserving and changing, as they move. It is not a simple binary process.[6] This can be mapped directly on to the term 'community', which both remains and changes, moves on and adheres, but is also is a kind of container of contradiction, which the term *'aufheben'* is, at root.

This is the dialectic I want to restore to Hegel, but much more importantly, I want to restore it to practical use, when walking around places such as this. Hegel's Logic is not 'common sense' logic. There is no binary separating of concepts in order to recombine them, as in a crude, three-part discourse. Contradictory, warring aspects of historical processes are migrating towards and away from the surface of one whole reality all the time. This is *'aufheben'*, but it is also social life as experienced in places such as this.

The other side of this theoretical re-figuring involves putting the *'aufheben'* back into Marx, who essentially described the *'aufheben'* of commodity fetishism, a phenomena which arises out of the elision of labour power, of the product appearing to arrive to us 'as made'. Marx explains how labour is evaporated in the commodity, how the 'process is extinguished in the product'.[7] Marx sees *'aufheben'* in the wider processes of capitalism, he sees that a sale is also a purchase, and a purchase is also a sale, but to talk about these small parts of the process is to pluck small instances out of the wider reality. He sees that this whole process contains internal contradictions, that it is dialectical. Capitalism is still a dominant organising principle of 'community', and this is also something of a Marxist project, and so a return to dialectical thinking became crucial to it.

4

Problematic dialectics

But I have perhaps explained this a little too neatly. I am returning to Hegel, and Marx, just after an era in which it seemed 'natural' to state that 'our entire epoch struggles to disengage itself' from Hegel.[8] Stronger sentiments have been extended to Marx, despite his recent Amazon sales spike. The Hegelian dialectic, '*aufheben*', carries some conceptual baggage, which is assumed to have sunk it already. But I want to work through that here, to lay aside some of the problematic elements before proceeding. In '*aufheben*', which Hegel really wanted to describe, rather than simple dialogues, we also have an excessively inflexible version of 'Truth', which we can see via Kojéve:

> Hegelian experience is a different story: it reveals concrete Reality, and reveals it without modifying or "perturbing" it. That is why, when this experience is described verbally, it represents a Truth in the strong sense of the term.

And here of we must pause, of course, as the whole history of structuralism and post-structuralism floods in, drowning Kojéve forever, and leaving only unidentifiable parts of the vast, monumental ruins of Hegel showing above the waterline, cracked and crumbling: We cannot begin to get to any form of truth without 'perturbing' that truth, without disturbing and re-constructing its 'truthness'.

Space doesn't allow a full reading of these philosophical debates, but I do need to explain what they destroyed: Hegel was the first, and as far as he was concerned, final, auditor-historian-philosopher. According to Kojéve, Hegel 'is content to observe and describe the dialectic which was effected throughout history, and he no longer needs to make a dialectic himself.' This is how Hegel's system is seen to be closed, finished, and this is exactly where I must distance myself from Hegel. But in distancing myself, I also want to properly re-open what was thought to have been closed. Because dialectical method itself is not submerged with the rest of the Hegelian ruins, it floats free, therefore it is always moving, and it can form a raft via which we might view the fragments on the surface.

Theodor Adorno's 1951 text *Minima Moralia*[9] both continues and critiques the work of Hegel. In his 'Dedication' he describes how, under post-war consumer capitalism, the Western person is a subject 'for-itself' but no longer 'in-itself'. A lifted-out, alienated life of consumption has emerged. Adorno is using terms from Hegel's *Phenomenology of Spirit*. Hegel claims that his dialectical method, *aufheben*, abhors 'anything isolated', and so Adorno thinks that Hegel might have scorned the fragmented, aphoristic form which *Minima Moralia* takes. Adorno thinks that this idea's time has passed though. Hegel's method attempted to get beyond 'being-for-itself' and to see the whole as truth, but later, Adorno inverts this, saying 'The whole is the false'.[10] Adorno wants to return to the personal-as-politics, retaining Hegel's revealing mind in desolation, but ditching Hegel's wider, macro project as 'liquidating the particular'. Adorno is clear though, his relation to Hegelian dialectics is itself dialectical:

This book forgets neither the system's claim to totality, which would suffer nothing to remain outside it, nor that it remonstrates against this claim...

Hegel, Adorno claims, does not respect his own demand to be 'in the world', rather than beyond it, 'to penetrate into the immanent content of the matter' to attain truth, the mind must face and dwell on the negative, the 'reflections on a damaged life' which form *Minima Moralia*'s subtitle. This is what I want to do here, and negative in these debates means both critical and transforming.

If the subject is smashed, then the aphorism, the fragment, is essential. I am going to argue that Adorno's words in the late 1940s are still highly relevant today, and it is only via the fragment, or 'trace', that we refigure epistemology in order to proceed in an age of still-unstoppable global capital. Adorno explains that the 'splinter in your eye is the best magnifying-glass.' These fragments of *Minima Moralia* tell us how to re-position our view of the world dialectically, and how to see it in pieces and through those pieces. It also tells us how to re-approach autoethnography, or rather the personal-as-politics, something which also connects with C. Wright Mills' idea of connecting private troubles with public issues.

In Hegelian 'absolute knowledge', the distinction between the universe-as-god and the universe-as-material is dissolved as finally irrelevant. For many, myself included, it is simply impossible to live there. It is unknowable in its fullness. But this does not necessarily stop us from comprehending flashes of illuminated fragments of something much larger than us in the night, nor doing so through a return to a revised form of dialectical method.

I don't want to try to blind you with theoretical exegesis to win an argument here. But I do want to explain that we need to find the limits of the practical dialectic, in the field – out there – to test and find out where its limits lie, and that I believe that this can produce useful work.

The view of self-consciousness as radically incomplete, emerging from post-structuralist discourse, denies Hegel his view of any kind of 'completed' form of man. This is correct. But conversely, this radically fragmented subject is precisely what returns me to the doing of dialectics, as a process, as a way of thinking. Of course many post-structuralists sought something like an expansion of the dialectic, but the political subject became too broken up by post-structuralism.

The excessive 'Truth' of Hegelianism, crumbled by the floods of various post- moments, does not stop the dialectic being a useful tool, and a particular kind of return to it can temper some of the excesses of post-structuralism. Dialectics have actually been denied as a kind of method, and claimed as a force of nature, but I do not buy this. Semiotics and anthropology go some way to characterising homo sapiens as mutators of meaning, as transformers, symbolisers, makers and imaginers: Homo negator. Here we have, I think, a practical way back into the 'doing' of dialectics. The researcher and philosopher do not escape being 'inside' these processes, nor do sociologists escape the social. In a sense then, I am putting forward a proposal that I, you, us, do dialectics again. A dialectics with no end in sight: Infinite (yet finite) semiosis, infinite (yet finite) dialectics. Meaning, or dialectal thinking, cannot ever be either final or infinite for a subject who judges, who is also tied to a mortal body. We cannot know infinity, temporally or spatially – a point which heretically ushers Kant back in – but it is crucial to state that meaning and dialectics will go on beyond us.[11] This is what Adorno urged us to undertake in *Negative Dialectics*, a dialectics let loose in permanent, but global revolution.[12]

I want to argue for a re-opened, unstable, radically unfinished form of dialectics, which can be grasped out in the world. An ad hoc dialectics, to combine with Jameson and Williams' ad hoc base-and-superstructure.[13] We need to go out there again, as writers, researchers, thinkers, or artists, and begin to follow the dialectic practically again. But to get to the point where the dialectic can start, the transparency of our existence in the world must be loosened by 'the trace'. This is how the dialectic is put in motion, and I want to describe what I mean by this next.

5

The trace

As I have already explained, I am from the town I am writing about, and being from that town does not guarantee a clearer view of it, if anything it risks that view being misted-over with romantic attachment. For the transparent or opaque nature of experience to be undermined, shaken, forced to reveal its prism-like nature, the human subject who judges must experience a 'trace' of something other. Therefore, for the dialectic to begin, the 'trace' must be present. There are many precedents for this kind of thinking: Benjamin's fragments of messianic time, or Barthes' use of the 'punctum' when viewing photographs, historical detail which can put into motion a whole set of other epiphanies. Fredric Jameson is a dialectical thinker who often uses detail to make other connections. This is not seminal. Some sort of 'trace', given different franchising terms, is touched upon by all of these thinkers, and many others, Derrida included.[14]

The 'trace' has become crucial to thinking through my subject. After trying to find a completely new unit of analysis for 'community', I came to the conclusion that it was as futile a search as the quest for the original language. The 'trace' is not the unit of analysis for my research, but it does loosen subjects from their contained units, putting the dialectic in play. We now need to move through the subject of the human world dialectically, and find a series of 'units', if we have to make our subjects unitary at all. The risk here is that the political subject may become too fragmented, but I think that in a world where solidities still evaporate, this is the only way to track that world, but we always need to account for the ways in which those processes affect everyday lives.

Recently, I interviewed a man called James who once worked

in IT for the Halifax Bank of Scotland (HBOS). He left just before the crash of 2008 hit, to set up a company who make and sell locally-produced cheese. He didn't see the crash coming, but says that in retrospect, 'some people knew something about all this.' The IT team, normally only concerned with day-to-day, internal operations, were suddenly given external 'entrepreneurial projects' to generate money, liquidity, just before a massive liquidity crisis. The IT people at HBOS were then restructured constantly, departmental names and job titles changed regularly, with a new set of business cards each time this happened. What turned out to be early symptoms of the crash – constant restructuring – caused James to seek other employment, other ways of life. When he left, James took these unused, irrelevant business cards from the bottom of his desk. James now labels his cheeses with his HBOS business cards. He uses their blank backs to add notes. These tiny little traces of history are very interesting. Not old, safe history – 'heritage' – but history still in play, history which cannot be put into a museum, precisely because its existence in space has not yet been tamed by time.

I suggested to James that re-using his business cards like this might be a nice little act of 'recuperation' and he enthusiastically agreed. Here also is redemption. This tiny trace is live history, as live as his new work, as live as his cheeses. This large quantity of business cards was literally produce by an oncoming crash, almost as though they were blowing in the storm Benjamin uses as a metaphor to describe modernity – an endless piling up of ruins.[15] More straightforwardly, James's new business, historically couched in the 'localism' of 2013, has been set up with money skimmed from a business bloating out of control in 2008. There is a very large historical juncture here, which plays out, not only in the very narrow valley I am researching, but also globally, and it is triggered by tiny details, 'traces'.

The return of the middle classes to localised production, re-occupying sites – literally in some cases – evacuated of working class life, is a return precisely to re-create the long sequence James has just witnessed a small part of. A sequence of small beginnings, large, slow swellings and rapid burstings. As these people move through these processes, they jettison or take on certain aspects of social class, agonistically, to bracket themselves off from others in the field, or to align themselves with others with whom they can work. Social class is no longer expressed through the slab-like dimensions of industrial life, but through individual details. It is in this way that people now try to root themselves in an inherently rootless world. These processes are not simple conversations, they are inherently contradictory, and those contradictions can never be simply separated off and examined. These hermeneutical spirals curve up into the night, peppered with the bright shards of historical fragmentation, which are turning dark and fading into the larger structure as we watch.

This return to dialectics, via the trace, is inextricably bound with, in fact requested by, the way that industrial capitalism has radiated outwards – globally – and then rebounded on the places which innovated industrial capitalism in its first phase, and here was such a place.

There are further traces of both this history and the way its exports have rebounded, which can be detected in the built environment. Not far from Scaitcliffe Hall, in Centre Vale Park, there is a statue of John Fielden, a mill owner. 'The Fieldens' were the biggest cotton dynasty in the town during the nineteenth century, paying for the construction of the park where the statue stands.

As an MP, Fielden was instrumental in getting the Ten Hour Act through Parliament. Yet the Fielden family have also been criticised for providing far too little too late for their workers, as they built vast, expensive monuments to their achievements, such as Todmorden town hall Here is a little of the local dialectic of industrial capitalism.[16]

In 2001, somebody, probably from nearby Todmorden High School, visited the John Fielden statue to paint a Nike 'swoosh' on his waistcoat and trousers. As Benjamin once wrote, 'no poem is intended for the reader' and this wasn't an exception. Intention is impossible to prove, but I suspect that the message may not have been about bad working conditions in this country, patriarchal rule, or sweatshops in South Korea, but simply a re-branding of something old, or 'square', using a logo, a 'cool' brand. But intention is not always important, and Benjamin's thoughts on poetry relate to the act of translation. This statue, with its swoosh, indicated the Northwest's shift from an innovative globaliser during the industrial age ('Just Do It'!) to a post-industrial, globalised region, importing its clothing from overseas. Here was the way that history had been exported, and had rebounded, symbolically, on the town.[17]

Here was another 'trace', which put a dialectic in motion, that illuminated the traffic between the micro of small towns and the macro narratives of a globalised world. Any claims about this macro picture, from the perspective of writers, researchers, or artists, must come from the micro, not the other way around. The dialectic is in the detail, or at least it begins with the detail, via the 'trace'.

As I returned to Todmorden again in March 2011, an attempt had been made to steal the John Fielden statue, which was incorrectly assumed to be made of bronze.[18] A little later, my parents' boiler packed up, and just before they could order a new one, the industrial unit in Mytholmroyd which produced them was broken into and cleaned out of its copper stocks. This business subsequently closed down. These details demand that community ethnography shifts its focus, not only to the concept of 'trace', but also to the wider contemporary situation, because the space of community isn't neatly bounded any more, in truth it never was, but under the loosening effects of globalisation, the idea of a 'site' has become so stretched that the term is probably no longer appropriate, conjuring up, as it does, fences and boundary lines. As we can see, the fluctuating global prices of raw materials are not some flickering, distant data sets, viewed on the screens of only those whose business it is to deal with them, they partly create the landscape on which everyone exists.

Some earlier research, undertaken in Todmorden by Amanda Ravetz, employed a multi-sited approach, which covered the council estate, farm, factory, and local agricultural show.[19] Though all these elements can still be found – the latter two being perhaps the least visible – it occurred to me early in my own research process that a multi-sited ethnography of the future would have to re-focus on the symbolic and real construction of 'here' and 'elsewhere', globally, and I will add to this my urge to account for it dialectically as well, in terms of its inherent contra-dictions.

For me, these are methodological, practical points, rather than philosophical, 'academic' ones. There is no single, discrete space of community any more, and the only way to respond to this is via a re-calibrated approach to the new practicalities of being in a landscape, coupled with a return to dialectical thinking. We need to move away from the concept of 'site' altogether and engage with an ethnography of 'trace'. 'Historical' place may now mean a house vacated by a worker from the Czech Republic, this morning, in order to return to the Czech Republic In ethno-graphic terms, it may not be practical to follow that worker, but we can find traces. It is possible to reconnect the surface of any given community with its multiple, hidden contexts, tracing interrelationships of people and things which are often thousands of miles apart, but are connected by the new temporal and spatial relationships I have just outlined. Objects became a good way of doing this, because objects are easily traceable, with their places of manufacture written on them. We don't need to go to China to see China Shipping, we can see the containers in freight yards locally, and en masse in nearby Manchester. But the trace of an accent and the overheard snippet of talk were equally important to the task of re-connecting distanciated relationships, and teasing out the hybrid nature of the contemporary social world, as well as the paradoxical, dialectical nature of social life.

We see this in social life all over the globe, and not just in places previously thought of as tucked-away, 'timewarp places'. Time and space have been 'flattened'[20], yet 'timewarp' is still a very useful word to raise, in order to think through what happened to life in post-industrial small towns such as these, but only if we hijack it and refigure it.

In one sense, my project is in the lineage of Raymond Williams, with his exploration of what 'experience' means.[21] But my own biography no longer unfolds much like others of my generation, so that both my experiences and theirs might inform an approach to the 'how' and 'why' of that unfolding. 'Experience' has irrevocably changed since Williams was writing, and I have attempted to translate his concerns – the ideas themselves – onto a vastly altered terrain. Of course, there are things, potentially, that we all share, and the fragmentation of bounded lives and linear narratives is one of them. Perhaps it is the only one.

The shift into a post-industrial, technologically-interconnected, globalised, postmodern era is the main reason why 'experience' is now different in Todmorden. The 'cliff face' generational bandwidth approach has become fragmented, mainly because what used to be geographically clustered working lives are now dispersed. My father and his friends lived in a place where industrial life was considered to be immortal. They then witnessed its unstoppable decline, and some of them ended up scratching a living from marginal, sometimes illegal or rather sketchy practices. I have already described the need to find public solutions to private troubles, which is what I am doing here, but it is also crucial to point out that those 'solutions' should not stop at the borders of the country we are in. Again, this is a risk of the close attachment to place I began to critique in my opening sections. The need to seek externally-facing solutions to internal problems should also begin to create an internationally-facing local. Making this methodological inversion is appropriate, because the little story about my dad and his mates also has its dialectical flipside, as Sarat Maharaj explains:

At the highpoint of industrial take-off during the first modernity, the coastal factories of India closed shop: technical know-how passes over to the increasingly mechanized Lancashire factories and mills. The Indian subcontinent experiences "cloth famine". In a second move subcontinental migrants arrive to bolster the dwindling Lancashire workforce or to buy off outdated, stripped industrial ware to set up shop "back home". With rise of the knowledge-based economy, Lancashire jobs are increasingly outsourced to India. The seesaw relations that underpin conjoined modernity are not only about step-by-step development: more crucially, they involve the haphazard and relentless "production of underdevelopment."

The 'stories' of Todmorden and India are two sides of a coin, they construct each other, the one is not possible without the other, they are and have always been dialectically meshed, an integrated assemblage, produced by capitalism and imperialism.[22] Yet small towns have been understood in the past as discretely bounded, framed by methodological nationalism, viewed through the lenses of a provincialism which has produced much that is negative in sociology as a whole, not just community research.[23] Again, there is much we can take from Adorno's *Negative Dialectics*[24] to inform this doing, but it is the doing I want to both encourage and turn to here, and not just by the priests of academia, but all who feel the splinter in their eye.

It may be tempting for some critics to accuse this move to

dialectical thinking via the 'trace' as a jump too far into cultural relativism, and perhaps a position of political shoulder-shrugging. But I believe that the direct opposite is the case, because if the only methodological unit left to us is the trace, this might actually tell us much about the socially fragmenting nature of late capitalism and global processes: We have to move like the thing we are trying to catch.

SMALL TOWNS, AUSTERE TIMES

6

Rural and urban, public and private

Raymond Williams revisited his book *The Country and the City* in 1984, identifying the urban crises of the time, including 'extreme cases of actual riots and burning'.[25] He measured these urban flashpoints against the crises – as he saw them – in rural landscapes, all of which tally quite strongly with the present, albeit with some marked differences: Williams highlighted agribusiness, the reduction of human work on the land and its flipside, the increased use of chemicals and machinery. He outlined how 'the rural' had changed, with country houses and mansions being presented as our national 'heritage', although some of those buildings were also occupied by 'leaders of City finance' back in 1984, only a few years away from 'the big bang'. Williams spoke of equitable green socialism, which, for him, must replace this mechanisation, as both agribusiness and industrial capitalism put profits before people and increased land values.

We will see that in my research location, many of the themes Williams spoke to in 1984 are still lividly present, a perceived need to return to organic, localised forms of production, but also the return of various nationalisms, and the return of a new provincialism which is actually underwritten by 'the radical'. Williams's comments are quite naïve and retro-facing I think, although this is not total by any means, as he argues for a 'return to community' in a later essay, and here he is very careful to add the caveat that localised, 'ground-in' community ties can also be used to exploit people in a very bad order.

At one point in his essay on *The Country and the City*, Williams re-affirms his point that country and city are 'indissolubly linked', a theme which he doesn't really develop in a satisfactory way. Here, I want to take that theme up again, dialectically, in order to develop further what he began. I want to explore how the rural has been raised in the image of a whitened set of histories, against an industrial background, but also to challenge how even within those historical collages, the rural and urban are misunderstood, and the discourses around them again present conceptual containers which are excessively binary.

Via this set of processes and their assumptions, emerging from nineteenth-century visions of industrial development, the rural and urban in northwestern towns such as Todmorden are also classed in various ways, with the rural assumed to be associated with 'posh' incomers, gentrification and country life, and what remains of 'the urban' – and much of this is processed through aesthetics – with work and the working classes, but also with crime and degeneracy. These attitudes may have been forged in Victorian times, but they are present in skewed ways in contemporary life: A local anti-supermarket campaigner, Dr Lindsay Smales[26] described the 'wrong' and right' visions of the town, 'wrong' being industrial units and 'right' being heritagised Victorian shopfronts covered in hanging baskets. Smales has essentially reproduced a tourist and heritage vision of the town, which can only fetishise industry when it is safely tamed by time, via its aestheticised relics. This illustrates that a distance of around fifty years is a rough, bargepole-touching length for heritage culture, but that this does not simply remain in museum and tourist industries, but saturates social assumptions locally.

The 'uneven development', which we can see in Todmorden back in the nineteenth century, via the Roger Birch archive[27], can still be seen now. It is this uneven development which visions such as Dr Smales' are produced through, essentially, when he says 'not industrial units', he unconsciously says 'not now'. In one hundred years, industrial units may be valued historical relics. Classed visions are placed in quite particular relations to time in order to do their work, their editing, their eliding: it is a redactive and slurring process which occurs. This does not end in big public planning projects, its logic rebounds into the construction of the privatised spaces of home, as I will explore later.

We can see the uneven development of the present: The site of a proposed marina and Sainsbury store in Todmorden is at the moment a stretch of derelict land, as supermarket planners competitively hedge against other supermarket planners. As the flood defences are being completed, they are being rendered redundant by more virulent floods, but more widely, there are stretches of derelict ex-industrial land all over Todmorden, the odd new and completed housing estate, next to crumbling and badly maintained terraces. The old cinema and the Abraham Ormerod Centre remain derelict, right in the focal heart of the town. Neil Smith[28] describes how the see-sawing motions of capitalism, boom and bust, can be tracked physically in cities by observing their dead zones and places of activity. I want to suggest here that the change in scale does not render Smith's advocacy irrelevant to small towns such as Todmorden, but further, that we can to an extent see in this infrastructural collage a map of the cultures and attitudes which sit upon them: A collage of rural and urban, past and present, modern and 'backwards', slow and fast, emerged during fieldwork.

With these examples in mind, I now want to describe how the rural and urban are constructed and elided in various discourses, but also how history is employed, by pulling it into the present in edited form. However, I want to show that very strong parallels can be detected between lives lived then and now, at the same time I want to question the legitimacy of those kinds of cosy comparisons. To begin to explore this complexity I want to start by outlining the love-hate relationship with Todmorden which emerged through different groups of people, another binary relationship which revealed other containers, the rural-urban particularly, but also the slow and fast, the boring and the exciting, which in turn were produced out of the cultural constructions of industrialization and therefore 'urbanization', which I have outlined above.

Todmorden has been re-designated a 'market town', something which has rural connotations. The town has had many of its key industrial sites erased, for instance Mons Mill. But more manufacturing remains than might be assumed. In many ways, Todmorden is still neither industrial nor rural, this argument can be made in relation to visions of the town in the nineteenth century, as well as in the present. However, Todmorden is certainly more of a rural site now than it was in the early twentieth century, it would be irrational to claim otherwise. This said, I want to argue here that the 'rural' or 'urban', as designated from above in a very binary manner, is not the point of a project such as this, but how those paradigms are still employed, constructed and re-constructed, in particular sets of ways by particular people, should be central to it.

Kane, who we will meet later, had a very strong sense of the visual 'rightness' or 'wrongness' of Todmorden, which emerged from his employment as a 3D artist. Kane described the relatively recent realisation that his home town is 'a beautiful place to live' in almost revelation-like terms. Many people of his age expressed similar things, for instance Helen, who explained that she hated Todmorden for a long time and thought of nothing but escape, but suddenly realised how beautiful it was and learned to enjoy it. Most of these explanations were couched in leaving and returning to the town, from locals who went away and came back, or incomers. I rarely heard this from someone who had never left. The landscape, when he was young, Kane explained, was so familiar that it was essentially transparent. Later, the people he worked with in Manchester told him 'you're really lucky to live out there'. Abid Hussain, who again we will meet later, also described his relationship to Todmorden as coming and going in six year cycles, from Britain to Pakistan, although these cycles have stopped now. He told me that he loved walking in the countryside and that 'there's no better place', when you're up on the hills, and that the landscape is beautiful. Again, he mirrored the words of Kane verbatim, saying 'you could go anywhere in the world' and struggle to find somewhere as beautiful as this.

But this love of the rural has its flipside. Later, when Kane described particular supermarket proposals as 'monstrous' or 'horrible', this early explanation of his relationship to the town as 'beautiful' — which aesthetics are central to — framed the details of his refusal. Yet Kane also described Todmorden as 'a kind of Royston Vasey', the town from The League of Gentlemen television comedy series, which is largely based on Hadfield near Glossop, although it was filmed around Stansfield Street in Todmorden at one point in 1999. The League of Gentlemen is a kind of gothic-noir-comedy, presenting a small northwestern town full of backward, perverted, often murderous characters. The League of Gentlemen presents an essentially rural hell, a kind of northern English version of southern American backwaters, and it draws on some of the horror of ultimately moralising films such as Deliverance. Kane occasionally displayed some disdain for 'blinkered' locals whose visions of the town didn't tally with his own, and this reference to 'Royston Vasey' seemed to lurk under those moments, along with traces of moralising. Kane described Royston Vasey and Todmorden as 'out in the sticks a bit' and I heard many other joking references to 'country bumpkins', 'yokels' and 'inbreds' during research. This said, Kane berated another user of the Todchat website page, dedicated to the marina campaign he is heavily involved with, for describing others as 'Royston Vasey', before effectively accusing her of a Royston Vasey mentality, for describing herself as Todmorden 'born and bred'. There was a kind of strange, looping logic to this: As soon as 'Roytson Vasey' became shorthand for 'backwards' forms of provincialism, people could be designated 'Royston Vasey', but then it seems that the designators could also be designated 'Royston Vasey', for designating it in the first place. This is the snake that eats its own tail, the Ouroboros of deracinated localism.

There is a real tension between these two explanations, of Todmorden as 'rubbish', but nonetheless home and homely. This can be traced right back through Amanda Ravetz's PhD on Todmorden and Jeanette Edwards work on nearby Bacup.[29] These further, binary judgements of 'good' and 'bad', were present throughout my time in Todmorden, particularly in young people: 'Tod's rubbish' and Tod's boring' or Tod's shit'. These statements would nearly always be left hanging – as if they were beyond obvious – but when pursued they would invariably lead into an essentially rural set of stigmas. So 'Tod's shit' was indissolubly linked with 'there's nowt here' which was always followed, roughly, by 'it's boring'. 'There's nowt to do' became a kind of mantra.

As we can see from the CCCS essay on 'doing nothing'[30], we cannot take these declarations as straightforward, and reproduce a common sense, naïve ethnographic account of them, because 'nowt' often means quite a lot of activity, and actually what they were explaining wasn't the lack of experience but the quality of their experiences. 'But it's very beautiful', I offered, on a few occasions, 'who cares', was the inevitable reply. Again, I think the response depended a great deal on whether the person in question had left and returned or not, but for many of these young people, the urban was exciting and Tod was 'full of old farts'.

These statements also, I think, had a classed dimension, as it was often working class young people who fetishised the urban as a place to gravitate to for an exciting life. In this sense, the nineteenth-century paradigms of rural leisure and urban work have collapsed. But what these assumptions of small places surrounded by countryside as boring or backwards or 'inbred' do is to reproduce nineteenth-century classifications of the urban as active and the countryside as slow.

Darren Smith's PhD on nearby Hebden Bridge[31] identified the attractions of 'the rural' for middle class incomers. These included the temporality of the place, re-producing a kind of rural weaver 'survivalism' on the hills, coupled with a commuter lifestyle to Leeds or Manchester. So we can see how the urban and rural have different appeals to different groups, but also, in this last example, how older forms of labour are being fetishised and re-occupied by particular groups, something I will explore further in relation to Todmorden. 'Survivalism' as a term to be applied to the well-off is inappropriate in light of some of the forms of 'getting by' I experienced here. This, I think, is completely tangled up with work, the key organiser of space and experience, and I want to turn briefly to that now.

7

Different temporalities of life and labour

I spoke to Jean, the DVD seller, who we will meet again later on, after he had been arrested. He essentially told me, almost the first thing he said, without of course using my language, that he missed the temporality of his practice. For Jean, a key benefit of his informal labour practice was managing his own time:

> ...the freedom, even though you do more hours, it's whatever you wanna do, and you can stop when you've reached what you need, you can work out that... that's enough now...

In this his practice shared much with mainstream freelance work, and I will later make a full case that for sociological purposes it should be viewed alongside those practices.

But there are other local historical parallels we might look to here, in order to explore the temporalities which frame these cultural differences. Heywood & Jennings[32] dip into the diary of William Greenwood, a handloom weaver who notices the passing seasons and weather. He works hard, but manages his own time, sometimes walking in the valley, watching the hunt and catching up on work later. That same year, 1825, Samuel Palmer completed his near-hallucinogenic 'Early Morning', exactly at the moment when such rustic cosiness – if it ever existed, which I doubt – was being inverted, transformed into a pursuit for the privileged, for the next century and a half at least. Despite some negotiation of her or his own time, the handloom weaver worked, indoors, during every moment of available light, the mullion windows in cottages were installed to optimise its spread.

Similarly, Jean worked in an attic space, in his terraced house rented from 'a bloke' he knows, 'plenty o' light' up there, he explained. Palmer's idea of a contented 'creature of nature' was created at the very moment of industrialization. Although Palmer and the romantics were ideologically opposed to industrialism, working 'all hours god sends' was a pre-condition for both the factory worker and the home worker: Palmer's entire concept is fake. The economic advantages of machine-owning entrepreneurs and the division of labour for the subsequent factory workers are the issue. Hannu Salmi points out[33] that the romantic yearning for a pastoral idyll, a pre-technological fantasy, had no influence on the political developments of its age, yet it continued to grip everyday emotions. Now, in Todmorden, as elsewhere, these 'everyday thoughts and feelings' include a recourse to a 1940s 'blitz spirit' a co-opting of naïve agrarianism, and other forms of habitus which are just the modern version of what Palmer was trying to do aesthetically, and the access to technology and different capitals are equally key drivers to class and experience.

What I am trying to explain by smashing these examples from the past into some from the present is that there is traffic between the lives spent now, the temporalities of their labour, the getting by and the not getting by, and my contemporary material. We need to be able to catch glimpses of the historical in current practices and vice versa, but we need to be very careful about how the cultural masks we meet on the surface of the landscape tend to cover the real nature of the lives there. This, in fact, is a large part of their purpose. The world of material change, 'progress', unstoppably transformed communities in the nineteenth century, as it is doing now, after the crash of 2008, in a different way.

But the wider point I am also making here is that the urban and rural are far from stable paradigms, to be applied top-down, they are created and re-created in different, classed, gendered, ethnically-othered ways, whether that be in physical spaces such as factories, home weaving operations in the nineteenth century,

Jean's illegal operation in 2008, or in cultural assumptions about Todmorden being 'slow', at the same time as essentially industrial operations still thrive, for example Warman's Engineering on Halifax Road, which uses just-in-time ordering processes which are very quick indeed, until, of course, demand trails off. Therefore, we need to revisit towns such as these and look for the variable speeds which can be found there, in different places, at different times, and the variations of rural and urban 'as declared' by the subjects, as essentially cultural garments, and then to try to account for the mosaic-like structure which will inevitably emerge from this.

8

Resolving speed via the public and private

In his essay, 'Time, Work-Discipline and Industrial Capitalism'[34] E.P. Thompson tracks the emergence of different figurations of time under industrial capitalism, pointing out that our understanding of it is not natural, and that it has developed historically. We were not born into it. Thompson cites Thomas Hardy:

> Tess started on her way up the dark and crooked lane or street not made for hasty progress; a street laid out before inches of land had value, and when one-handed clocks sufficiently subdivided the day.

He then lays out how the instrumentalisation of time begins to unstoppably enter every sphere of existence in the west:

> As the seventeenth century moves on the image of clock-work extends, until, with Newton, it has engrossed the universe. And by the middle of the eighteenth century (if we are to trust Sterne) the clock had penetrated to more intimate levels.

To explain this last point, Thompson simply shows us Tristram Shandy's father, obsessively winding the clock in the house, as though his very life depended on it. It could perhaps be argued that it did. In the nineteenth century, Thompson points out, 'the clock is sometimes known as "the devil's mill."' He then cites Evans-Pritchard, contrasting this emerging, re-constructed understanding of time in the industrial era, with that of other cultures during the same period, who had very different relationships with time:

...the Nuer have no expression equivalent to "time" in our language, and they cannot, therefore, as we can, speak of time as though it were something actual, which passes, can be wasted, can be saved, and so forth. I do not think that they ever experience the same feeling of fighting against time or of having to co-ordinate activities with an abstract passage of time because their points of reference are mainly the activities themselves, which are generally of a leisurely character. Events follow a logical order, but they are not controlled by an abstract system, there being no autonomous points of reference to which activities have to conform with precision. Nuer are fortunate.

This geographical point is important: The past and present are concepts that are perhaps more straightforwardly 'of time', but the 'rural' and 'urban' also call on different figurations of temporality, both cultural and actual. They also often call into play notions of the authentic and inauthentic. So here are a further set of binary concepts – albeit ones emerging from the assumptions of our own era – which become entangled with the subject of time and speed.

I want to argue here that fast and slow, past and present, urban and rural, are all concepts which are tangled up with each other in complex ways, they are not binary or neatly separable. This idea is applicable to the past of the nineteenth century, as much as it is to our present day. I want to work through some of the excessively neat binaries here, in order to show how those binaries don't really hold water.

Ultimately though, I want to argue that the public and private are the ultimate, dominant paradigms in which many of these binaries are actually resolved. The public and private can decide speed, and the public and private, of course, are directly figured by and through our age of capitalism.

In Chethams music school in Manchester, it is possible to visit the old library, founded in 1653, where Marx and Engels wrote, and stare out of the windows at the high rises like new factory chimneys. A list of what they read lies on a lectern. This includes *Description of the Country from Thirty and Forty Miles around Manchester* by John Aiken.[35] The Aiken book reveals that Marx and Engels were reading about the upper Calder Valley and its cotton production:

> No exertions of the masters or workmen could have answered the demands of trade without the introduction of spinning machines... These machines exhibit in their construction an aggregate of clock-maker's work and machinery most wonderful to behold. The cotton to be spun is introduced through three sets of rollers, so governed by the clock-work, that the set which first receives the cotton makes so many revolutions than the next in order, and these more than the last which feed the spindles...

Here is a description which is associated with new urban life, but the upper Calder Valley, where this scene took place, is viewed as fundamentally rural, and so I want to argue that this assumed relationship between time and space, of speed with the urban, of slowness with the rural, are actually warping and weaving relationships. This kind of practice was not fundamentally 'of' the urban, tiny Todmorden held the biggest weaving shed in Europe.

It is also possible to return to the nineteenth century which E.P. Thompson deals with, to begin to further undermine these neat, over-easy notions of time, moving in an 'upwards curve', through 'development'. To do this, it is possible to access photographic archives which show this largest weaving shed in Europe sat next to roads where farmyard animals wandered. Here is one simple way in which the binary walls between rural and urban crumble, and in photographs of a road a few minutes walk from this huge weaving shed, we can see rural slums straight out of Rider Haggard, at the height of industrial modernization. Pavements began to arrive around 1908, fairly late. Photographic evidence shows that the emergence from a rural space was relatively slow, despite the enormous changes all around. Older technologies, such as the grindstone, were still in use here during the nineteenth century, the sand from it being used instead of carpets, in farmhouses and pubs.

So, we can go back and see the future arriving, but at the same time we can see that some very antiquated elements of past practices survived a long way into that future. This begins to question excessively neat productions of the urban and rural and to illustrate that uneven development can be seen throughout all periods. Again, we may want to add 'uneven decline' to this, in the dialectical spirit of this work. In a nineteenth-century image of Rochdale Road, we can see that telegraph wires and electricity cables are starting to reverse the material-industrial infrastructure, as chickens wander in the middle of the street. Marshall McLuhan, in *Understanding Media* (1964) describes how Marx based his work on the machine, just as the telegraph began to reverse the mechanical dynamic.

In his recent book, *A Guide to the New Ruins of Great Britain* (2011) Owen Hatherley begins his chapter on the West Riding of Yorkshire by describing Will Alsop's proposed Supercity, which was to connect vast swathes of the northwest up along the M62 corridor. This vein is crucial to the region as a whole. Go and stand on the footbridge across the M62, just above Littleborough, and inside the relentless roar of hundreds of droning lorries and screaming businessmen, you may scry David Harvey's voice, explaining how the movement of capital cannot ever stop, not even for a nanosecond. You may even feel, as I did later, that you need to look up the details of the journey to be made with Charon across limbo into the world of the dead. This spot arches back to the nineteenth century, as on nearby Blackstone Edge, the

Chartists gathered to try to put the brakes on a modernity which was flattening them. As we can see, their success was mixed.

But then later, standing outside the Midland Hotel in Bradford at night, what was amazing about this nearby city was how deserted the streets were. The cars at this point were as frequent as donkey carts in tiny Tuscan towns, despite their steaming out of the centre during the rush hour with some of the relentless violence of the M62. It is also possible to stand on the moors at night and watch the planes circling to drop into Manchester Airport, and see the communication beacons covered in red lights. One cannot see this in the day, and only investigators such as myself would go to those completely unlit places at night.

The point I want to make here is that temporality is as crucial to our age as it was in the industrial era, but our understanding of it tends to be a default one, it is 'pasted in': the urban is fast, the countryside is slow, but none of this is as straightforward as we might think. All those neat binary paradigms are overlapping, we cannot simply apply, for instance, the urban and rural onto whole swathes of land or populations, top down, we have to work through what is there, in an ad hoc, reflexive way, contrasting the rural 'as declared' with its constructed, un-natural-ness, and vice versa.

Speed, the urban and rural, past and present, are not neatly contained now, and via my previous examples, hopefully, it is possible to understand that they never were.

But one thing combines them all, as I have already hinted, and that is capitalism, the public and private. In cities, our current recession means that temporality responds not to circulating capital, but to its lack. Mark Rainey and I[36] wrote about the still, silent construction cranes, in relation to post-slump Manchester. Rainey also describes the Sharp Project on Oldham Road, which co-opts public infrastructure for private ventures. So the public and private are not neat, binary categories either, and via this example Rainey points to the development of Silicon Valley via ex-military infrastructure. This is crucial to understand in relation to right wing media discourses which are currently pitting public sector workers against private sector workers, as the public sector continues to take industrial action, and from many conversations in the town, I can declare that the right wing media discourses are working.

But in Todmorden the deadness or busyness of spaces in town are still largely constructed by the deployment and retraction of global capital, particularly in the still-ongoing supermarket debates. There is a dialectic to be accessed here, not a simple linear narrative. Yet the global view of Todmorden, accessed outside the town via media discourses, often gives the sense that the town is constructed and reconstructed by benign, holistic localists. A very big point of this book is to question these and similar narratives and return to the complexities of their real, dialectic natures.

Even the default histories of industrialism tend to conceal its fundamentally dialectical nature: In Walsden, just up the road from Todmorden, we can visit the site where John Cockroft grew up, one of the trio who first split the atom. His family owned Birks Mill and Birks House, and their industrial cotton business taught John how to undertake large-scale electrical engineering, fixing lights to dynamos powered by the factory water wheel, and it allowed him to go to Manchester and then Cambridge where he eventually split the atom with Rutherford and Walton. In this we have the leap from water wheel technology into the nuclear era, via the industrial age, in one single generation, through one figure. Cockroft's work also altered our perception of time, making atomic clocks possible, and in this he is the caveat E.P. Thompson would need to add to his essay on temporality and the industrial age, were he alive to do so. I have written about this elsewhere.[37]

My own great grandfather, returning from the first industrial war, worked an almost medieval practice of tenanted small-scale farming, right next to this space – Birks Mill – which effectively incubated the atomic future, one which was visualised in the 1950s as all shiny space-suits and hover-bikes. In fact, my great grandfather was given permission by the Cockroft family to work this discarded scrap of land they owned, right next to the water wheel, as they busied themselves with visits to complicated science talks in Cambridge. He occasionally worked as what he described as 'a handyman' at Birks.

This stands, I think, as a metaphor for much that I have to say here, about the mis-understood, excessively neat descriptions of the rural and urban, the 'backwards' and 'modern', but also about the public and private, ways in which lives in small places like this are not 'all connected up', as one might be tempted to believe from outside, reading localist rhetoric about the town. Here, we are presented with micro-universes next door which never really meet, although they may be aware of each other and in touch. This description is mistakenly associated with the urban, and not the rural, but further, it is also mistakenly associated with the present and not the past.

My great grandfather's need for a very different kind of temporality, after experiencing that of the first total machine war, was provided for by the private, not the public. And I want this also to stand as a metaphor for some of my concerns here, as I fully believe that this is now the final binary in which all the others are settled, and it is also the final set of binaries which must be eroded and destroyed.

My great grandfather was a recipient of some paternalistic benevolence, but now one must pay to not work by working. This is the final double-bind, the knot in which all of these other messy concepts are finally tied: It is possible to drive from Oldham, over the moorland road to Huddersfield, a town with a largely ignored, poverty-stricken demographic, via a place called Delph, where we can see the Porsches and scaffolding of what is essentially a massive moorland gentrification exercise. Here is how urban and rural, past and present, slow and fast, really count in all of this – this is the geography – it all gets resolved in the other constructed binary of the public and private in places such as Delph. If you drive for long enough around the main roads and more modern bypasses you will eventually be led up one of those roads you have to come back down to go anywhere else, at the end of which you will find the privileged elite.

This argument, then, is about how money doesn't circulate and re-circulate, but how it congeals in pools, and when it does so, the rural, slow, and 'the traditional', another fake epistemology, is raised to naturalise this recent influx of very new cash. It is also raised to exclude the other, and there is nothing slow about the cars, or the speed they drive, in and out of their gated-by-default communities.

In the urban zones in and around Rochdale — where child poverty has reached half of the population in places — rural enclaves like Delph provide a distorted mirror image, because the urban zones in Rochdale are 'economically necessary' to the creation and continued existence of Delph. Because Delph's Porsches and cranes are paid for by the lack of capital re-circulating only a short drive away, in the urban slump zones surrounding Manchester, a place nonetheless still within a single Porsche's reach. And of course this is Delph, but above Todmorden on Blackstone Edge, in Heptonstall, and Mankinholes – a tiny place which saw the start of one of the plug-pulling riots in the nineteenth century – exactly the same thing has happened.

This, finally, is how speed figures: in the circulation or lack of circulation of capital, in the power of transport to bypass slump zones on the way to a place which is disingenuously constructed on an everyday basis as 'slow', 'traditional', 'rural', and 'natural'.

9

Rural, urban, Empire

To return to the essay by Raymond Williams I opened this section with, particularly his unfinished question about the links between the rural and urban, I want to state again here that the rural and urban are indissolubly linked, but both are fetishised by the processes of enlightenment rationality and capitalism, philosophical and technical approaches which separated them out in order to control them in the first place, and continue to do so, albeit in a decentralised way. When Abid and others from the Asian community in Todmorden talk of walking up above Centre Vale Park in their Shalwar Qameez' and trainers, I think about the money flowing into the Fielden brothers accounts from cotton production which enmeshed India and the Americas in their processes.

I thought about this every time I walked by the John Fielden statue, with its Nike 'swoosh' – which itself signifies speed – painted on his waistcoat and trousers. This money paid for the statue, and the vast, oversized park in which Abid now walks. The park is enmeshed with the Empire in the early eighteenth century and the exploits of the British East India Company. The park, so fundamentally 'local', and spoken about in those terms, is global and hybrid. But this hybridity is difficult to see, unless one takes it apart almost forensically, as I have tried to do here. Abid is walking in and around something which has been paid for by flows of capital from these 'other' places and processes, but which is still declared quintessentially English, a paradigm of English ruralism, and yet the park takes its aesthetic and architectural influences from, variously, Italy, Germany, and Greece.

Yet Abid himself is endlessly othered by everyday discourse in Todmorden. Abid is not an 'anomaly' in the landscape of the park, as was suggested to me at several points during fieldwork, but is dialectically connected, historically, to the site, via colonialism, empire and the flow of capital during the industrial revolution, at the same time as he is also dialectically at odds with the utterly spurious notions of 'Englishness' in the park, as are the Gilbert Bayes statues to the dead of WWI, which process Greek classicism through medieval arts and crafts aesthetics, proto-modernism. Everything here is dialectically both in and out of place. This is an argument about *here*, of course, this park, but it also stands as a metaphor for my argument about the practice of going to small towns and being in them, in order to write about them, about small town ethnography in a 'local' which can do nothing other than hold a set of contradictions, conceptually. We need to pick up on these traces and allow them to start their dialectical processes.

But to pick out Abid as an example is to both highlight the bad epistemologies which still stand on these landscapes, at the same time as it risks reproducing those very same epistemologies. Everything here is hybrid, everything, not just figures on the landscape singled out by potentially racist cultural practices: I attended a Todmorden Labour party meeting where the Asda store was being discussed. A councillor explained that the Asda plans were more 'in keeping' with the town than the Sainsbury's plans, as they utilised the Deco-esque Modern cinema building. I put forward my opinion that none of it was in keeping with anything, and the Deco Modern building only seemed 'natural' because of the amount of time it had been there. My argument wasn't really met. In this, we can see how blind assumptions get coded into town planning. When I spoke to Kane, who works on 3D visualisations of 'the local', he told me that he was trying to 'weather' his projection graphic for a supermarket near Hebden Bridge, in a kind of aesthetic fait accompli, to make it look like it had been there for a long time, in an illustration of something which had never been there, and may not ever be there.

There is a direct practical relationship between practices of everyday life deemed to be 'urban': wearying back breaking factory work in noxious environments made of blackened brick; and the fresh air and health of nature associated with 'the rural'. These relationships were and still are part of everyday life. My father's recollections veer between descriptions of hellish labour in brickyards and factories full of cotton dust, and moments spent undertaking seasonal agricultural work, and this work is within both official and unofficial economies, which I shall later dialectically fold back into the single paradigm of 'getting by'. He told me that:

> We used to spend time at Grandad Newall's hen-pen, his first one was just over the bridge from Knowsley Avenue. He used to keep hens and also Grandad and his son Jack used to share pigs. They used to fatten them up, and when they reached a certain size they were slaughtered for meat. One particular year, in winter, when the canal was iced over, one of the pigs escaped and got onto the ice. Grandad called the fire brigade to see if they could get to it with their ladders. But before they arrived, the pig fell through the ice. When they arrived, they spent time breaking the ice trying to locate the pig. But it was too late, the pig had drowned. It made headlines in the Tod Rag [Todmorden News and Advertiser] but sadly it was only worth half of the value it would have been if it had been slaughtered. Grandad had put a lot of work into rearing it, he used to go down to Todmorden market to pick up all the cabbage leaves and food rejected by the greengrocers on the stalls, so it was a great loss to them.

He then went on to explain that:

> Another job we did on Sunday was potato picking in Knutsford, Cheshire, for Reuben Ratcliffe. We used to set off

early mornings on the back of a covered wagon. On our way we used to stop at a slaughterhouse in Rochdale and pick up milk churns filled with horse's blood, this was to mix with the food Reuben fed his Turkeys with. He was renowned for the quality of his "Top o' th' Hill" Turkeys, as they were known. We used to also call off at the Café Royal Hotel to deliver a batch of freshly killed Turkeys. Killed on the farm above the Hollins pub. The potato picking was backbreaking work, but it gave us some much-needed pocket money.

Here we can see that the urban and rural were relatively – a key word to use – meshed paradigms during the industrial era. This is not a new insight, but what I am building towards here is the idea that the rural and urban only make sense as separate and separated spheres of activity if we look at the way in which they are being employed, dogmatically, to sell something, property, a lifestyle product, or to resist incomers, or demarcate oneself from the other. It is to these things that we must hold as community researchers in places like Todmorden.

To be clear, I am not making some overly-dogmatic Marxist table-thumping argument here, I am trying to relativise all these binary paradigms without losing the sense of inequality, of uneven development and decline: The rural is a space for the leisured rich, but it is also the place where the alcoholics go to escape the pressures of life; In Jez Lewis's film on nearby Hebden Bridge[38] and Paul Barker's book on the town[39] many drinkers can be found in the park, and they can be found up lanes and behind the Park Woods in Todmorden, but they can also be found around by-products of 'the industrial', for instance the canal system which has now been turned into a leisure space. So here we have middle class tourism and underclass escape using the same space, and they never meet. In fact, I want to argue here that they pass through each other like ghosts. Theses spaces are liminal, mixed, spliced, stratified, something associated with the urban, yet they are often presented as holistic, knowable, more local, cosy, of 'the rural'. We need to constantly question these epistemologies and there is often never an easy answer to the questioning.

So what I really want to argue here is that the rural and urban are such fudged canisters that we should lose them completely, in favour of examining how the rural and urban are raised agonistically within the local, and linked to 'the local' as an agonistic trope, by various agencies on the landscape. Trying to create indexes and typologies of 'the rural' is a completely pointless undertaking which should be left in Ronald Frankenberg's taxonomies in 'Communities in Britain'. But these assumptions don't remain in the 1960s and 1970s: Michael Woods' Rural Geography[40] asks why we should bother with the rural at all, but then concludes that we need to keep it as a straightforward container, because it has a 'deep' history and because governments employ it as a paradigm: I have argued against reproducing dominant epistemologies all the way through this book, and here is no different. The 'depth' Woods raises is actually only surface complexity, and we need to resist these essentialising philosophical statements. The rural is as contested a container as 'community'. My cynical alertness always 'switched on' when the double figure of 'rural community' was raised linguistically, by any group, which is essentially a singular and reifying term made from two imaginary ones. Darren Smith[41] also struggles to define what rural is, in a chapter in his thesis. We need to simply move on to rural or urban – as with community – as declared, before asking by whom and in what order?

What is often under these declarations is revanchism, the gaining of resources, and on the flipside the resistance of capitalist processes, and these are what should concern us as community researchers. To return to Smith:

Subsequently, the relatively less affluent indigenous house-holds have been displaced from the location or marginalized to the less desirable parts of the location. If development is spread geographically, then the negative effects need to be taken into account within any new proposals. The 'processes of revitalization' must minimize the detrimental effect on the indigenous inhabitants.

I don't much like Smith's use of a supposedly straightforward paradigm called 'the indigenous' either, as social researchers dealing with 'community' in a post-community context, we must reject any authentic containers of rural or urban – or even past and present – as well as incomer and insider – although we should have a keener, more heightened sense of the temporalities of different lives lived in the landscape, and the way that the insidious knots of public and private include and exclude. People are isolated and overstretched here in very polarised ways, and in this we need to be concerned about how 'backwards' and 'slow' or 'fast', and 'industrial' (or not) things have become, but for specific spaces and groups. These paradigms cannot be declared top-down in some macro fashion, reproducing naïve descriptions of community which also often emerge from the communities themselves.

We then need to find, through dialectical processing, the fault lines, the fissures where ideology is being soldered, and to show this.

Returning to the public and private

But we should not stop here, because what is really crucial, to return to Williams's advocacy at the start of this section, is to reconnect the urban-rural axis properly, sociologically, away from some of the mushy idealisms encountered in everyday life, some of which Williams himself has been (to my mind, incorrectly) accused of.

In January I went to a party at a house within Hollingwood, a private estate consisting of very large expensive houses, just outside Todmorden. It wouldn't be strictly correct to call Hollingwood a 'gated comunity', there is no gate per se, but the road leading up to these homes is private – signs point this out – and the houses are far removed from the public thoroughfare. The architectural aesthetic of these new homes is a kind of Yorkshire ruralism arriving via Los Angeles. As I walked on to the estate and up the road, I witnessed a nasty spat when a car tried to park. A big red family vehicle with a sliding side door pulled up behind another, and someone got out. There was some conversation, which I couldn't make out as I was too far away, but as I got closer I heard the woman who had just got out tell the other woman who had just parked to 'shift it', very abruptly. She then stomped back into her vehicle and drove past. There seemed to be no blockage to complain about in the first place, the red family bus got past easily on the wide private road, the whole thing was like a scene from Godard's *Weekend*.

I continued up the drive. Inside, I greeted my friend's family. The woman who had just been told to shift her car followed behind me. She explained what had happened, and the wife of the man who owned the house we were in asked her, 'was she a fat ugly bitch?' They all laughed. Once the formalities were over, we waited for my friend to arrive, and as we did this, I looked around, intrigued. I turned a corner to discover that the owners had built a pub inside their house. The only indication that this may exist before walking into it were a number of fridges in corridors on the way there. In fact, fridges seemed to be everywhere. Aesthetically, the interior was that of a modern popular hotel, perhaps a chintzy version of Travelodge. They had attempted to create what Mike Savage might call an 'enchanted landscape' for themselves[42] but Savage doesn't fully figure the way that is always raised agonistically into his account, something which is crucial to re-include if one is to describe what is happening in places such as these properly. The heightened competitiveness of the working classes who had 'risen up' by creating excesses of available cash were on display at every turn during the evening. That competitiveness did not rest, or become 'holistic', once it had achieved wealth, it turned outwards to compete with the other, the 'fat ugly bitch' down the road, and in this it might reasonably be claimed that a 'disenchanted landscape' can also be identified, whether or not it has access to economic capital. Yet the money for this haven began to accumulate via informal economies, before that money was 'legitimised'. We shall see a failed attempt to do this in Todmorden later. Outside the metropolitan centres, this is perhaps an inevitable form of 'resourcefulness' for many.

So again, these things are always dialectical, never simple or straightforward. The rural aesthetic of Hollingwood also acts as a container for other binaries, the public and private, which, as we can see, are equally blurred: The hotel, a place where public bodies make themselves private, is invoked in the interior decor, which is perhaps appropriate to the function of the building, and to the symbolic aspirations of the owners, but the pub is usually a space where private bodies make themselves public. Perhaps, here, it should be re-titled a 'Priv'. This may not be a 'gated community' in the strict sense of that term, but some of the logic of gated social life festers there. The public house in this sense was an oxymoron. It wasn't built to be a place where strangers could meet. It took the form and aesthetics of what is in those places – basically all its commodities for the individual – and then puts them beyond the reach of strangers, although strangers can see them on rare open days such as these. We can perhaps contrast this with the widely reported 'death of the pub' all over the northwest, and it is possible to see pubs in every town steel-shuttered and empty, Todmorden included.

A mutual friend of mine had brought his partner to the party, a woman with Bengali roots. Curry had been laid on, and the women who made the comment about the 'fat ugly bitch' down the road were careful to coo about this guest, picking her out, wince-makingly saying 'isn't the coloured girl lovely', to the other guests. Here is provincialism, a perhaps unconscious part of their habitus, but that habitus also partly consists of this priva-tised, fakely traditional rural, and it also contains this cultural unconscious, which casually regurgitates its othering in 'isn't the coloured girl lovely'. Proclaiming that 'we're not racist here' actually involves undressing so that everyone can see the racist tattoos underneath your clothes.

Much more broadly speaking, this was not a 'public house', far from it. Of course, this was one occasion when people were invited in, otherwise I would not know it existed, but there was an excess of concern about who was coming, before the party, and how the owners would know who was in their house, partic-ularly in terms of people bringing their own partners. Behind the 'pub' was a hot tub, California-style, but in an area which has some of the highest rainfall statistics in England, and forty minutes drive away, one in two children reckoned to be in a state of poverty. The house across has two indoor swimming pools. I felt that some of Setha Low's concerns could be seen in the nasty spat before I arrived, that private, inward-looking life doesn't bring psychological security, quite the opposite.[43] There is a 'proper' gated community, Lakewood, at nearby Hollingworth Lake – even closer to Rochdale, race hate and alarming statistics – but the logic of 'gatedness' also saturates the long line of houses all the way down the valley, some of which have enclosed themselves cheaply and conspicuously.

Later on at the party, I chatted with a few smokers outside the front door, where the conversation loosened up. A relative of the family who owned the house was there, a woman from Rochdale. She had a thin, pinched face which seemed to speak of poverty and struggle. She started to express her worries about the economic climate, to me and a friend. I immediately, without thinking, started to talk about politics. She suddenly started to cry. I stopped talking. She apologised for crying, 'I hardly know you', she said, suddenly embarrassed. She continued to explain her circumstances, living in Rochdale, trying to bring up her sons in a rough area. She said that she wasn't worried for herself, but for her boys, '…what will they do now? There are no jobs. And then I come here…' She stopped herself. I felt the tension between the party venue and her life, but this tension couldn't be spoken, it wasn't part of the social occasion. But I could tell she felt it, and that she understood that I felt it too. This woman didn't know how well I knew the people at the party – the people in her own family – and I didn't know how well she regarded them. She didn't know where my friend sat on the issues which began to arise, and kept looking at him nervously, after she became upset. The wealth gap was right there, but it was unspeakable, even in a supposedly intimate, family and friends situation.

This is how the dialectics of the public and private play out – the dialectics of deracinated localism – on top of the rural and urban, old and new, slow and fast, in provincial, small towns.

So what, I wondered, is the opposite to this space? I realised, ultimately, there wasn't one: I spent a night in what is described locally as 'the anarchist house' in Todmorden. This happened because I bumped into Billy one evening, an ex-heroin addict from my year in the local High School, who did some time in prison for holding up a post office with a knife, when he was desperate for drug money. Billy had just returned from Greece. He told me that he had seen the 'anarchist dog' there, a dog which barks at riot police, and 'someone cooking up smack in a doorway'. He was with a new girlfriend. We had a drink and caught up. Closing time loomed and they invited me back to the house for a drink, so I went along, curious. The 'anarchist house' is a very big terrace in the centre of town. We went in by the back door, past three old guys with long grey hair, the elder anarchists, who nodded sagely. Billy led us to the large communal attic space, which was full of people. Youngsters were up late, drinking White Lightning cider, but they were also treated as adults, they were having adult conversations. Joints were also being passed around and someone was face down, having passed out in the middle of the space.

After a little while I managed to reveal that the house was owned outright by one of the anarchist elders. Eventually I got tired and asked where I could sleep. Billy made a grand gesture by explaining, loudly, that 'you can sleep anywhere man, go find.' I walked out of the attic space, down some stairs, along a corridor, and then I turned into the first room I came across, where I was faced by a man with long grey hair, writing at a desk. 'This is my room!' he yelled, irate. This anecdote almost works like a joke, but actually, I think there are some very serious points to be made with it: The gated house with its own pub has turned a space where private bodies make themselves public into one in which public bodies privatise themselves by returning to the home which has inverted the logic of public life. This logic can be tracked on the wider landscape, for instance in the conversion of the Free Trade hall in nearby Manchester with its history of private bodies making themselves radically public – the suffragettes, the Sex Pistols, Bob Dylan – into a Radisson SAS hotel, where public bodies now make themselves expensively private. As it does this, it converts radical history into commodity, something which can be seen more locally in the co-opting of Co-ops and vegetarianism which have roots in nineteenth-century Manchester liberalism.[44] The point I am making with this material is that these processes are not confined to cities and city culture, but can be seen in small town community life in places such as Todmorden, as we shall see.

The anarchist house has attempted to re-invert the logic of the gated community by keeping 'open house', and I don't think that my slightly awry view of my experience there actually changes the fact that the status of 'open house' is being seriously attempted and to some limited extent achieved. However, the anarchist house exists within the capitalist logic of property ownership, it cannot exist outside of that logic. So here, returning to my dialectical theme, are a set of concepts which contain each other, it would be tempting to arrive on this landscape and declare the provincial enclave with its own pub, and the anarchist squat, with its communal attic with bottles of cider, the diametric opposite of each other, to declare something along the lines of Frankenberg's 'morphological continuum'[45] but this would be to provide an inflexible account which would ultimately break; the public and private, rural and urban, do not figure along this kind of continuum, like a mark on a ruler, nor do the past and present.

These phenomena need to be handled dialectically, as concepts which contain their opposites, and each other, in distorted, positive and negative mirror images of each other. Here I have tried to provide my first set of proposals around what characterises the dialectics of 'deracinated localism'. It has provided the broadest framing of the concept, as I needed, initially, to set out the ways in which the rural and urban are figured in places such as Todmorden: The rural and urban are not binary spaces to be travelled in and out of, but flickering concepts raised culturally, often to exclude or exclusivise. Via these concepts, I want to show the ways in which all the people on this 'local' landscape sit on a wider landscape of capitalism, of flows of goods, money and services, or their intermittency. But this wider landscape is so wide that one cannot navigate around it, so high that it cannot be climbed over. Because of its vast dimensions, it also cannot be seen by many people here – it cannot be seen 'in the local' – and yet attempts to make instinctive defensive gestures against 'it', symbolically, in raising the signifiers of an utterly fake, whitened rural history, as well as actual gated spaces, is being attempted by many of the figures and groups I encountered.

As we will see, this is key to 'deracinated localism', as is the intimate situation which conceals the suffering of the other, something which sometimes even includes close family members. This was not an anomalous situation in Todmorden. This is 'deracinated localism', it begins with the big, macro divorces of global power from local politics, a rift so vast that it cannot be viewed from the ground, and it saturates all micro-social relations here. But as I will go on to show, Todmorden is so often presented as *more* friendly, *more* spiritual, *more* holistic, *more* 'of' community, and *more* intimate, than other small towns, and certainly more than cities. 'Deracinated localism' is a framing concept which can erode these mythified version of place – there is 'localism', it says, its discourses can be strongly located – but it will always be an uprooted localism, at the same time as it assesses those mythifications as essential to daily life, and acknowledges that those myths are blamelessly experienced by the subjects of this research 'as natural.'

This is the point where strongly reflexive empiricism arrives, looking from outside, at a point where one can see the contradictory assemblages at play, at the same time as their 'natural' everydayness is also understood. That the researcher is sometimes caught within the same double binds is also acknowledged.

From this broad framing of the concept of 'deracinated localism', and some of its dialectical movements, I want to focus in a little closer now, to describe how people 'get by' in Todmorden, descriptions which I also want to erode mythified versions of Todmorden, as either filled simplistically with the feckless unemployed, or the thrifty 'getters on' of the middle class volunteers I will examine later.

THE DIALECTICS
OF DERACINATED LOCALISM

11

Epistemology

I have already explained my main aim in sections 1-5, which is to shift the boundaries of community research, literally and epistemologically. We can view community research as a kind of genre, with all its previously described limits, some of which are also literal boundaries: the community as the local-only, geographically-bounded, timeless, generalised and generalisable, explainable in causal terms, etc. If we take the criticisms of community studies as a subject seriously – and I do – then its genre must shift, by creating a new approach and exemplifying it.

All my talk of shifting boundaries can be mapped – if only metaphorically or poetically – onto what happened to real communities just before and after the twenty-first century. If one problem has been that small towns were presented as discrete, frozen, centralised and timeless, the solution must be strategies which deliver pluralistic accounts of spaces which are much less bounded, at the same time as the social remnants of that boundedness can be found. To do that, the craft of community ethnography and its representational strategies must be re-calibrated to the task again. We need to be able to detect traces of the global in the local, but that isn't all, because the global isn't always fully showing in places such as Todmorden. So the other aspect to this 'opening-up' of the craft must involve seeing 'community' as holding a set of contradictions at all levels, contradictions often produced by an inability to see the wider picture.

As community researchers, we should resist the temptation to declare *a priori* designated zones in small towns, such as 'the factory' or 'the council estate', and not just because they bring connotational baggage, linguistically, but because they are not discrete units, geographically. So I have avoided themes which reproduce these tropes.

We also need to avoid making 'common sense' into theory by accessing the social world through naïve ethnographic accounts, we cannot simply take what our subjects say at face value and communicate this, as there are layers of latent and manifest content there, and these layers are not easily separable. This is not to say that 'the factory' or 'the council estate' are taboo terms, never to be spoken, but that any social 'containers' must be declared by the subjects of the research, not the researcher, they must emerge from ethnographic description, after which an understanding of the way their assumptions function can be analytically generated, a multi-sided perspective. This is actually the point at which we might begin to re-assert containers such as 'the factory' and 'the council estate' again, as symbolically declared by our subjects, demarcated in particular ways, rather than easy containers of meaning which a researcher might set up and loosely fill with description, as many traditional community researchers did.

Here, to begin to address my ambitions, I want to focus on the line between work and non-work, official and unofficial economies, in order to explore the place where post-industrial life is experienced. Factories still account for more of a share of the employment in Todmorden than I would have assumed before taking up fieldwork.[46] But practical necessity forces me to focus on the main elements of my title, on the 'deracinated localism' to be found in Todmorden. It isn't completely impossible to give an overview of all the working practices of the town in one chapter, but it would be impossible to do that and do justice to the kind of community ethnography I am making a case for as well. 'Place' is a misleading term to use, as the zone of experience I am describing exists between the cracks of 'official' economies or a state of permanence. Of course, this is un-representative in some ways, as the town isn't completely made up of criminal or semi-criminal entrepreneurs, far from it, crime is relatively low in the upper Calder Valley, compared with the lower area. However, like the anarchist house and the gated enclave, I want to argue here that these kinds of unofficial cultural practices provide a distorted mirror image of the on-off, discontinuous, often fugitive expectations of the *official* labour market in post-industrial towns, they act as a striking metaphor for the qualities of everyday life.

I also want to argue that focusing on this line is necessary in light of the oncoming economic landscape, and will continue to be necessary long after the snapshot of this moment, in this place, has been rendered irrelevant. In this sense I also want this section to exemplify the kind of approaches to discontinuous working lives, ones which are 'on the border', in this border town, that I think are going to be necessary in the current, wider historical context, very soon.

Of course, as soon as one starts to talk about 'discontinuity', the discourses emerging from Bourdieu on 'precarité' rise up. Mario Candeias[47] explains how 'standard employment' is disappearing, by which he means continuous work patterns with strong rights, organised in trade unions. What was known as the 'proletariat' have morphed, and Candeias sees two new groups emerging, a 'precariat' and a 'cyberteriat'. The 'cyberteriat' are 'highly qualified, flexible individuals, working in short-term projects', they 'are sceptical towards unionism or refuse it' and they are characterised by their technological proficiency. The flipside is 'a sub-proletariat in insecure labour relations and with low income', which Candeias calls the 'precariat'. Candeias is clear that precarité:

...is not a problem of some small groups outside normal unionised labour relations, not even of the mass of global (labouring) poor. Rather, precarisation is a general process to dismantle and polarise the levels of social rights and standards of living, with very contradictory consequences, for most of the labour force, including the highly-qualified cyber-tariat and the old proletariat...

As I write, the coalition government are discussing the further de-regulation of labour markets, to furious opposition from the trade unions, who are attempting to show that the arguments made by ministers which supposedly prove that de-regulation stimulates employment and growth are bunk. The trade unions are using labour research statistics to make their case, but if 'precarité' is to be located, qualitatively and historically – which is my project – it must be found in individuals working at the edge of the industrial and post-industrial, and at the borderlines of official and unofficial economies.

The main example I want to provide here is that of Jean, a man who worked in factories for some time, before reverting to what are classed as criminal activities, selling counterfeit DVDs, when that work dried up. He is currently attempting to 'go straight' and in this we have a full cycle through an unofficial economy and back into official ones.

I largely agree with Candeias's explanation of precarité, but I also want to argue that in the example of Jean we have the 'precariat' and 'cybertariat' rolled into one. We have a localised practice, which relies on global and local flows, as well as flows between formal, underground and household economies. His practice used information technology locally, to navigate global markets to source raw materials, and those raw materials largely came from newly industrialised nations such as China. His downloading also sourced illegal packets of data, globally, in order to assemble the digital content of his products into a package of globally-sourced parts, boxes from China and sleeves created using printer cartridges from Europe.

So, locating these practices is a more complex business than simply designating those who 'do technology' and those who don't. Locating precarité itself can be difficult, often there are problems even arriving at stable conclusions. For instance, in 'Fragmented careers – a study of Bristol labour markets'[48] Fenton & Dermott discussed the seam between those in relatively long-term employment and the fragmentary experiences of those in temporary, increasingly short-term employment. When concluding, they admitted that they could not provide a firm link between narratives of 'the disorganised and disturbing qualities of contemporary work' and their data, as 'most of the work histories were relatively continuous'.

The point at which Fenton & Dermott honourably admit their lack of a conclusion is the place where I begin, and I want to qualitatively explore precisely what they could not seem to weigh. This said, I will begin with a few statistics, to try to place Todmorden in terms of employment and unemployment, but also to critique the logic of ONS epistemologies, before moving on to my main ethnographic example.

12

The dialectics of working and not working

The first thing to say is that, overall, 66% of the population of the town are listed as 'economically active' in Todmorden, and 33% 'economically inactive', which means that the state classes roughly a third of the town as not economically active. But there are problems with listing, for instance, 'looking after a home/family' as 'economically inactive', not only from a feminist perspective, but from a Marxist one, as it can, and I believe should, be argued that much of the 'economically inactive' category conceals the labour which reproduces the 66% of those who are 'economically active' every day. The figure given for those 'looking after a home/family' is 6%, which is course is completely erroneous if one takes into account the amount of those reproducing labour, feeding and cleaning for other workers, children, etc, who are also working themselves.[49]

This said, what is fairly clear here is that the wages being brought in from what flows of capital there are through this part of the Calder Valley is still relatively small, whatever objections I may raise over the way the data is presented, again, see my General Introduction here for an overview of this.

But this point maps on to working practices more generally, a point made by Pahl, for instance[50]: For many people in Todmorden, the state of work and non-work isn't necessarily divided neatly into periods of official employment and time claiming benefits. The most frequent discourses focussed on 'getting by' in ad hoc ways, whether in one of these more official categories – 'signing on' or employed. Pahl's analysis still holds I think, I have a litany of individual and household testimony to 'making ends meet', 'scratching by', 'getting on with it as best we can', 'doing whatever we need to do', etc.

Insights such as these made by Pahl, which can be seen every day in Todmorden, coupled with ONS statistics which essentially reproduce nineteenth century divisions of labour, have partly forced the shape of this chapter, as I want to dialectically dissolve the fake, state barrier between official and unofficial economic activity. Again, I take much from Restivo's[51] argument that anarchism and social science can be fused to challenge domineering, 'archic' epistemologies such as these. But making this onslaught upon the binary nature of working and not-working, official and unofficial economies, the division of labour, technological and untechnological workers, global and local workers, and official and unofficial workers, also speaks to the dialectical method I want to re-inject into community research, and therefore sociology per se: These paradigms and people are all dialectically connected, they all contain each other as part of a wider assemblage.

I have already pointed out that unofficial economies are in some ways unrepresentative pictures of working practices in Todmorden. However, people practicing second economies weren't ever difficult to find either. For instance, I spoke to Peter, a man in his late 60s, who has now officially retired from factory work, but up until a few years ago earned what he called 'good money' on a 'pop round', essentially an unmarked van full of fizzy drinks and sweets, which he sold door-to-door.[52] He also had an informal trade in bicycles, but this was much less regular, and occasionally he would produce designer goods at very low prices, 'no questions asked'. When I spoke to him, he had some expensive walking gear, on sale for £5 an item, regardless of its form, walking trousers and jackets were all the same price. Peter sometimes referred to his round as 'hooky', which meant that it was un-taxed and occasionally turned up items of sketchy origin. It was interesting to me in light of the argument I have just made, that Peter ran his round when he was doing official work and when he was not. Sometimes he did both, and during some short periods, he did neither.

So, for a little while we talked about Peter's working life, which mapped onto the experience of many other men of his age, my father included, in that he had worked in heavy industry in one way or another until the late 1980s, at which point he got by as best he could, and his wife's income as a schoolteacher covered a lot of the gaps, and in this he had 'been lucky'. In his case though, there was a less clear sense of class narrative and social capital, in that his wife's essentially middle class earnings were fusing with Peter's 'hooky' ones, they were congealing in a single household.

Suddenly, unprompted, Peter then told me about the people he called 'the scrotes', which is an abbreviation of 'scrotum'. With this unlovely term he designated those in and around Todmorden and Bacup he sold drinks and sweets to, people who were claiming Income Support or Incapacity Benefit. Peter often expressed disgust at their living conditions, and this tirade often then stalked away from Todmorden, to search for victims further afield:

> There's a hot dog stand at Accrington, and at bloody nine o'clock in the morning they're eating that rubbish, and I'm thinking "why are they not working!" And I'm bloody one of 'em! And there's me and trying to keep fit… and them buggers not doing any exercise…

In his last line, Peter was referring to a recent hip replacement. He felt resentful about the out-of-work, but guilty about not working himself, despite being beyond pensionable age. When I spoke to him, Peter often processed a kind of guilt about no longer being employed, through these observations of others not working, it was a regular theme which emerged when talking to him, but also many other working class people of all ages who I encountered in the town. People would then sketch cultural resentments about others in, over the top of their own practices, at the same time as there seemed to be little difference between them and the people they criticised, at least to an outsider's eye.

There was a sense of resentment in Peter that, although he had kept himself physically fit throughout his life – he had been a keen cyclist and marathon runner – he was still experiencing problems in old age. Again, these resentments were sometimes aimed at 'the scrotes', or 'the slobs', another term of distinction he used. There was a link between the white, male, embodied working practices of industrial life in all of this, and the idea of keeping yourself fit and getting on with work, a practice which has been subsequently undermined on any post-industrial landscape. Peter, and many other men of that generation, were clearly attempting to control their own bodies through exercise, in a highly Spartan way, to control the one aspect of their lives they 'owned' in the chaotic landscape of post-industrial capital.

But Peter never seemed to arrive at this conclusion, he always remained in a relatively small circuit of explanation, a 'them and me' mentality. But when this rigid set of demarcations Peter puts in place are logically addressed, they collapse. Because far from being simplistically disgusted by 'the scrotes', Peter seemed fascinated by them. In fact, at one point I felt like giving him my notebook, as his descriptions were becoming sociological. Yet there was a detached mix of horror and fascination in his voice when he described them – and I'm not trying to claim that this is always absent from a sociologist's mind because 'they're sociologists' – but Peter seemed split between some sort of misguided jealousy, because these 'others' have experienced long stretches of time without having to go to work, and his perception of them as 'scroungers and spongers.' There was a contradiction here, as he was selling cheap food and other items to 'the scrotes' while accusing them of indolence.

One could describe this as 'hypocritical', but I don't think that simple hypocrisy ever fully accounts for the multiple functions of social practices or language. What was being experienced in these moments were the cultural ramifications of post-industrialism, the way the superstructure – culture – calibrates itself to deal with the base, or rather the discontinuous nature of the base, sometimes in a good order, but in this case, not so good. But we shouldn't place arbitrary borderlines between base and superstructure either, for they are meshed together.[53] Todmorden is a border town, and that border is geographical, it is the line where Yorkshire and Lancashire meets, although culturally, this line is often treated as the place where those counties *refuse* to meet. This seems to map, metaphorically on to the points I am making here through my ethnography: subjective and ideological lines were constantly being blurred by people such as Peter. Ultimately, he was refusing to let his identity merge with these 'others', and yet the landscape on which he moved meant crossing the border between himself and 'them', the other, all the time. Put simply, Peter had to place himself closer to 'the scrotes' through necessity, at the same time as he distanced himself from them. His attempt to draw distinction inevitably threw up contradictions on such a small-scale symbolic landscape. Again, there was a dialectic in play here, in which Peter and 'the scrotes' contained each other at the same time as they were bracketed apart. 'Dialectical' is perhaps too soft a term in light of the almost vampiric nature of some of Peter's interactions with the inhabitants of Todmorden and Bacup council estates, but nonetheless, this encounter spoke to my dialectical theme of deracinated localism. This point applies to most of the people and community groups I subsequently engaged with, Incredible Edible Todmorden, the Asian community, and the local neo-Nazi, what they all shared was this attempt to other and bracket themselves apart on a small-scale geography.

To take this idea further, but also to return it to the theme of this chapter, a similar dialectic is put in motion by interrogating the line between official and unofficial economies, as well as local and global flows, traces of material, objects, capital, and symbolic culture in the landscape. The slightly sweaty, disturbing quality of living inside these experiences – of trying to remain binary when those binaries don't hold – could nearly always be detected when speaking to the people accounting for them. It was perhaps what Althusser called 'interpellation', the point at which encounters with otherness uncanilly reveal the constructed nature of subjectivity.[54]

I became very interested in the use of the phrase 'on and off', which arose again and again during fieldwork, it alerted me to the precariousness of everyday life. 'How is work?' 'On and off' [Nicola]. Or, 'I live with me girlfriend, she's scouse, we've been at it eleven years, on and off' [Tony].[55] Linguistically, the permanent was often couched in the temporary, and vice versa. This again highlights the dialectical nature of contemporary community. This way of speaking seemed to have simultaneously replaced and subsumed older statements, such as 'up and down'. 'Up and down' designates a continuum, a rollercoaster-like one, perhaps, but 'on and off', a phrase which also maps good and bad, also assumes a fundamentally dis-continuous set of experiences. There was a generational aspect to this, terms such as 'donkey's years', designating 'a long time', via the image of a work animal – which my father still uses in everyday speech – seemed to have been replaced by phrases which signify discontinuity.

I wanted to speak to Peter further, but that was the last I saw of him. I suspect that he realised he had given me enough risky material to take back to what he described as 'them clever bastards' in universities. His disappearance wasn't too much of a problem, as I encountered the same mix of resentment and resistance repeatedly in Todmorden. These resentments and resistances, work and the state of not-working, have to be viewed as much more entangled, dialectical paradigms. As we can see through the example of Peter, cultural class and social capital in

73

the sociology of work must be considered in a similar dialectical manner. This idea shoots through much of the sociology of work, but I want to explicitly re-inject those accounts with the sense of a fully dialectical landscape, on which all of these supposedly binary paradigms contain each other.

Practically, this 'tangling' occurs when what used to be the 'traditional' white working classes try to root themselves in a landscape of labour which is fundamentally rootless. Again, this is not new. They have been trying to do this for several decades now. Their attempts to sink this taproot into permanent nourishment – security – will very often lead to an uprooting, and when it does, this process produces resentment. But those resentments cannot be neatly separated out from the resistance, and often neither can attempts to create security be neatly separated out from the chaotic lives lived in post-industrial landscapes. I also want to argue here that this phenomenon is what collapses the binary between people working in official and unofficial economies. Ethically, as sociologists, we need to re-focus our attention on to the practices of 'getting by' and away from criminology and the default epistemologies of 'justice'.

Time and time again, the narrative of a life lived in precarious and insecure circumstances surfaced when I spoke to the 'regular' workers who were supposed to be immune from the causes of those narratives: I talked to a man who lived in Todmorden, but who worked freelance for a single institution, just outside Halifax. He had line managers, as in a 'traditional' job, but none of the stability or security a traditional job brings. He explained how he got all the down sides of working for a company, being dictated to, being treated 'like I'm their property' [Michael, 2011] but none of the benefits, no personnel department to deal with tax or National Insurance, no regular hours and zero job security. Often he turned up on the days he was supposed to work to find the people running the project were at another site, at which point he simply had to go home unpaid, having spent just under ten pounds in transport costs.

There is no longer a stable paradigm called 'regular hours'. The few times he mentioned the problems they were simply brushed off. He felt that he had little real recourse to complain, precisely because of his precarious employment status, and there was a scary, locked-in aspect to this. There was a kind of stifled fury under his comments, all the more shocking because of its stifling, and a kind of sick tautology in his fear of complaining, precisely because his links with his employer were so tenuous. This man, in his mid-40s, was working in an 'official' economy – it could in many ways be described as 'white collar' – but one which had cut him 'free' of its securities. Again this is a precarité argument, and Richard Sennett's[56] explorations of the new corporate work ethic is key to it, as Britain and America put in place horizontal, laissez-faire networks, which replace the old vertical hierarchies. Michael had experienced the old model, working at Mons Mill when it was producing for John Deere, and the new model, and he wanted to go back to the old way of working, in fact he seemed desperate for its impossible return.

I reached a point where 'criminal' practices, and examples such as this one, seemed to merge. We need to be very careful with comparisons such as this, but at the same time, as writers, we need to refuse to account for the practices of working lives within the neat, official, binary categories, laid down by, for instance, the Department for Work and Pensions, or HM Revenue and Customs. The lines created by the epistemologies of tax and dole are not 'norms', they are not natural, they are policed cultural barriers, but they often appear invisible, or 'naturalised'. As qualitative community researchers, we should hold to the experiences of those on the landscape we encounter, and in the case of Michael, and Jean, the example I am about to recount, their experiences are more similar than they are different.

The kind of stifled fury and inward-facing resentment I

experienced in Michael could be found all over working class Todmorden, and often people seemed short of terms to express it. If there is something actually able to take root here fully, unfortunately it seems to be this. I heard similar stories, from barmaids in a local pub who turned up for shifts to be told to go back home again, having spent bus fare to get there. These girls were in their late teens and their expectations were being formed by this cultural mean, it was becoming 'natural'. A young man on the train station platform grumbled to anyone who would listen about how he didn't want to go to work, how he was on a lower rate for the first thirty hours each week, working conditions which, according to his testimony, sounded illegal. He seemed utterly disillusioned and was barely into his twenties. If we think about 'roots', which has a rather comforting nature connotation, it should also be in this sense. Some people are rooted early on in processes which only nourish them meanly, and there is a further, gendered dimension to this kind of labour, which continues. There is a dialectic of roots to be found here, which Amanda Ravetz[57] accounted for well – even though she did not use the term 'dialectics' – when she described working class Todmorden women and their description of the town as 'shit', not a place of quality, and yet at the same time 'home'. Nothing has arrived in the intervening years to substantially alter Ravetz's analysis.

So, to the 'emasculation' of previously patriarchal labour markets we must add the analysis provided by Mittin, who states that 'women's work is everywhere associated with part-time work, low pay and labour market segregation'. Hyman, Scholarios & Baldry hint at work pressure as a factor for both marital and relationship breakdown, or perhaps the reason for living singly in the first place.[58] This is how lives are lived under deracinated localism. The tendency to turn-inwards is strong, and therefore these stories risk remaining untold, becoming repressed, becoming, eventually, symptoms.

The 'hidden injuries of class' are becoming hard-wired into

the landscape. I very rarely heard an economic analysis of this situation from the subjects of research, not that I expected one. I heard lots of stoical acceptance and antagonistic outbursts directed at the unemployed, much more than I heard their situation being blamed on the ethnic other, although I heard this too. I also spoke to men complaining that their girlfriends lived with their mothers, when they lived outside the familial unit, paying a price they couldn't really afford in order to do so. Many were bitter about the lack of access to their children. One was about to have a solicitor he could not really afford send a letter out [Gary, 2011], and I spoke to women who were entrenched in work and looking after their young, bearing the largest brunt of the costs, both economically and personally, convinced that the male species was fundamentally aberrant [Nicola, Jayne, Amber and Yvonne, 2011].

I also heard many ill-informed remarks about single parent mothers. Of all lone parents in Todmorden, the majority are female, 339 households out of 371, but 25% are in full-time employment and 28% in part-time. Single mothers account for 2.2 per cent of the population here, but 53% of them are working, which makes roughly just over one percent of the total population who are unemployed single mothers.[59] This, of course, did not stop the comments from coming, and the local neo-Nazi posted many comments on his blog about 'slut mums'. I had a conversation with someone who made the same argument, who, when I asked him what he thought the percentage of single parent unemployed women was here, he told me that he guessed 'seventy percent'. Many of the people proclaiming these assumptions shared key symptoms: mis-directed anger, followed by a retreat to a clearly troubled accep-tance, neither state being able to articulate what was happening to the whole psychic organism. They work, but their work often doesn't work in the way they think it should. There was something of Beckett in this. But once this work isn't working properly, they very often don't interrogate 'the state of work', but instead deploy the same irrational arguments that we heard from Peter at the start of this section.

This literary reference may seem absurd – Samuel Beckett – but pathos, tragedy, and comedy were never far from the surface of my reading of the practices of a man who tried to straddle all the binaries put in place by the state, and therefore to disappear from their surveillance. Unfortunately, by attempting this, he eventually placed himself right at the centre of their attention.

My main substantive section here describes the practices of someone who was 'up and down', 'on and off' at all times, who tried to remain officially registered in work, while undertaking unofficial economic activities. In this, he became a kind of cipher for precarité, and for the state of life in post-industrial small towns, which I have tried to outline in my introductory sections here.

13

Jean, the DVD seller

I want to present an overview of a large portion of fieldwork now, in order to reinforce and exemplify some of the ideas I opened with. The relative openness and honesty Jean extended to me during my fieldwork was one benefit of 'insiderness', although I have already explained some of the problems with this kind of excessive closeness and assumptions around 'knowing'. Ward[60] states that:

> Sitting down with an active drug seller, or burglar with pen poised ready to record detail of illicit operations, has the potential to close a study down before it has even begun.

I had a very different experience to that, but I also discovered that some things were being filtered out during my dialogue with Jean, and some of these things will remain filtered out for ethical reasons: As I write, his problems are far from over.

I met Jean regularly, and followed him through his routines, sometimes staying at his house. Often, I would meet up with him in The Duke of York, a pub in Todmorden with 'a reputation', according to local myth. Jean almost invariably wears faded jeans and a t-shirt. He is forty years old, but dresses like the twenty-somethings in and around the pubs of Todmorden. He has a friendly manner and a cheeky laugh. Jean went to the local high school where he excelled at Maths and Physics, and was a county league chess champion and team captain. After taking his A-levels, he enrolled at Loughborough University to study pure maths, but failed the course in his first year, not attending lectures at all in favour of drinking heavily and taking the low-grade LSD which was in circulation at the time. He was thrown off the course, but given the opportunity to return the following year, to begin again. He did return, but repeated the behaviour which effectively failed him the year before, and so was finally expelled.

After a few years claiming Income Support, Jean worked at Mons Mill, making wiring parts for John Deere tractors, on a Fordist assembly line: rotating boards on which the same wire is repeatedly connected all day. Mons Mill closed when the work was moved to the far East. I also worked at Mons Mill for a short period of time – around six months – putting together the boards on which the wiring 'harnesses' were assembled, with colour-coded diagrams. This is where I first got to know Jean, although I knew of him from my school days. When Mons Mill closed, Jean then got a job at ABC Chemicals, on Halifax Road, for five years. This was mainly manual labour, but he eventually managed to negotiate a role in which he could make very limited use of his outstanding capacity for mathematical calculations. He left four years ago because of bullying management. Since then, he has been selling counterfeit DVDs in pubs. 'I'm my own boss now', he says.

Jean gets the content for the DVDs and CDs he sells by using peer-to-peer software such as eDonkey. He needs a lot of raw materials: fast computers, printers, printing ink, paper, CD stickers, blank DVDs, CDs and their cases. He used to get raw materials from a wholesale outlet called Bowler's, in Manchester, but he now orders nearly all his supplies online, as it is cheaper. Everything he sells is priced in denominations of pounds and fifty pence. There is a pragmatic aspect to this. He carries two very big bags of DVDs with him, around a fairly wide radius of the town, so taking a lot of heavy change is not really an option, plus he likes the exchanges of money and DVDs to be fast. He will trim money off DVDs if people buy multiples, rounding the price down fifty pence, or a pound or so, to a ten or twenty pound note.

14

Putting the practice in context

I want to pause here, to begin to frame what is happening, theoretically. Ray Pahl[61] describes the links between the first and second economy, as cash traverses the borders between the household economy, the formal economy and the underground economy. Pahl is clear that these practices 'are all responses to overall processes of capital accumulation.' He also points out that all economies rely on the amount of cash for redistribution, both formal and informal. These are crucial points to hold on to, if we wish to collapse the binaries between official and unofficial economies.

Jason Rutter and Jo Bryce[62] have carried out quantitative research on the consumers of counterfeit goods, a practice which has a history at least as long as currency and market-systems. Rutter and Bryce explain the impact of the practice on businesses, including:

> ...claims made by Trading Standards that in the north-west of England counterfeit goods cost legitimate businesses around £750 million and resulted in approximately 1000 job losses in 2003...

But Rutter and Bryce also argue that counterfeiting should be placed within everyday routines and a context of normal consumption patterns – the social world – rather than a criminological perspective, and their research shows that DVD purchase in pubs is the most likely arena of sale in the UK. This squares very strongly with my experience of DVD piracy here, as well as my own refusal to explain the phenomena through the lenses of surveillance. It becomes clear from reading Rutter and Bryce's work that a wide range of goods are counterfeited, watches, sunglasses, pharmaceuticals, toys, software, alcohol and even aeroplane parts. However, Rutter and Bryce state that previous research on counterfeiting placed it in economic terms, which often made sweeping links to arms, drugs and people trafficking. They say that:

> In popular discourse, academic research and trade association awareness campaigns, the consumer of counterfeit goods is frequently constructed as "other". In industry and policy they are represented as outside accepted everyday experience – as part of a criminal or technological underworld or a terrorist organization, as socially isolated, morally corrupt or part of a subversive subculture.

This was melodramatically and morally depicted in video adverts funded by the F.A.C.T. agency of the 1990s, which portrayed a kind of 'counterfeiter hell', with glowing brand-irons and logos, which burst into flames at the end of the advert. Rutter and Bryce point out that for the trade associations which fund such adverts, there is a vested interest in portraying counterfeiters as 'deviant' and 'criminal', to raise the profile of their problem and assist conviction.

Jean spends roughly a quarter of his time out in the pubs selling and another three quarters at home making up discs using household PCs, DVD writers and printing equipment. In this, again, he is both what Candieas calls the 'precariat' and 'cyberteriat'. The very rigid binary between the two which Candieas employs, does not hold.

The other mythical figure which is often raised in relation to DVD piracy is 'the hacker', as a kind of anti-capitalist gremlin. Rutter and Bryce challenge this stereotype of the purchaser of counterfeit goods as a kind of post-*No Logo* consumer. The 'computer geek' image is raised to place the consumer of counterfeit media products in a normal-abnormal relationship: 'normality' being the purchaser of 'genuine' branded goods. Rutter and Bryce want to move beyond these myths and situate the consumers of counterfeit goods into '...a more routine and situated practice of consumption.'

This seems sensible, and having spent a long time out with Jean, I would also challenge these myths as applied to the producer of counterfeit goods as inevitably part of a large-scale mafia-style operation, encompassing other criminal activities, or the 'slippery slope' towards them, or as some sort of subversive anti-capitalist activity:

> ...for the majority of users, the advocacy of counterfeiting is not anti-capitalist but instead a variation of pro-capitalist consumption...

I would also add to this any temptation to place the practice under a full post-industrial excuse though, which legitimises criminality through labour market statistics. Jean has entered this practice because work was scarce and its qualities disappointing, but he clearly has a maverick streak too, and occasionally sounds like a Thatcherite businessman, describing his 'core market' and talking about 'new product' as essential to 'driving business'. He is effectively an entrepreneur.

But I also want to tack on a further caveat here, that, despite wishing to align myself with Rutter and Bryce's urge to place this kind of counterfeiting within everyday life, care must also be taken not to de-emphasise the risk to the counterfeiter, which their profession brings. It became clear during my time with Jean that he has become increasingly removed from the world of tax and national insurance, as well as the property rental market, which increasingly subjects potential tenants to credit and employment history checks, which often resemble a criminal investigation. Jean rents his house from 'a bloke' he knows. This said, he claims to have spoken to a major corporate mortgage lender and frankly explained what he does – and that he has several thousand pounds capital – after which they anecdotally told him that he would be eligible for a mortgage. If this is true, it immediately bolsters the idea of flows between official and unofficial economies, and further undermines the binary separations made by business and the state.

So there is a complexity here, rather than a simplistic relation, which needs to be accounted for. Jean often describes the 'easy life', which can often be had via his practice, at the same time as he sometimes veers into anxieties over the illegality – and therefore risk – which is the flipside to this 'easiness'. These are some of the inherent contradictions to his practice.

The DVDs Jean takes out to sell are all recent Hollywood Blockbusters. Today he has multiple copies of *Centurion* and *Toy Story 3*, among other 'big name' films. He regularly checks magazines such as *Empire*, as well as online film review sites, and only downloads and produces films which are given 'a six out of ten star-rating', at least. This is a global-local practice. He is often very honest when customers ask him about the quality of the films, giving his own frank opinion when he has seen something, but didn't enjoy it, and admitting when he hasn't seen one of the films he is selling. Jean loves film and considers it something of an informal subject of study.

Rutter and Bryce tease out the social dimensions in the exchanges of counterfeit goods further, citing the desire to see 'the latest soonest', as high on the agenda of counterfeit DVD film consumers, something I see clearly in Jean's practice as a producer. He takes great pride in staying up to date with the Hollywood movie industry, seeking out the films as soon as a 'torrent' is online (a packet of download instructions). Jean talks of his 'customer base', and of 'sourcing fresh products' every week, much like a mainstream retailer. He needs to get hold of the latest Hollywood blockbusters, preferably before release, as this creates an aura of exclusivity, which, as he puts it, 'shifts the discs' in the pubs.

In pulling the subject away from its usual place in criminology, Rutter and Bryce examine who buys counterfeit goods, rather than who makes or sells them. Again, this part of Jean's extended network was crucial to understanding his practice. I watched Jean selling several different DVDs on Friday to essentially queues of people, most of whom told him they were staying in on Saturday and Sunday and were buying their entertainment for both evenings. 'That's my weekend sorted' was a mantra of sorts when following Jean. Again, the purchases are stimulated by economic scarcity, and this squares with Pahl's comments about how the formal and informal economies are linked and framed by both an availability of cash in the system and the privation caused by capital accumulation more widely.[63]

I watched a grandmother buy a copy of *Toy Story 3* for her granddaughter in The York, as the child's mother played the bandit, and a young man buying a Peter Kay DVD for his father. Jean tells me that his busiest time is Christmas, and that he begins his own Christmas shopping in October, as he is constantly producing and selling across November and December. Again, the black market very closely mirrors the mainstream or 'legitimate' market, with its adherence to big-selling blockbuster films, but also the usual cultural events such as Christmas, summer holidays, and in this sense I think Jean is undertaking seasonal work of a sort.

I felt that these scenes proved the need to collapse the binary between social life spent in these places and the forms of social life able to purchase DVDs in HMV or through Amazon, but often this wasn't reflected in Jean's own attitudes, and he occasionally lapsed into the kind of paradoxical attitude we saw in Peter at the start of this chapter: Sometimes Jean would describe his winter round as 'Christmas presents for the Chavs.' Yet a colleague in a local art college, where I worked throughout this study, after meeting Jean, suddenly exclaimed 'who was that Chav?' The signifiers of class couldn't often be seen by those who wore them, and they flickered in and out of register, from viewer to viewer. Jean though, to be clear, had a much more sociable, friendly relation with his customers than Peter did. He genuinely seemed to like them all, yet these comments weren't simply an unconscious dimension of his habitus either, they were deliberate, though joking. There was a Janus-faced relationship here, as he made comments like this to me, he bracketed himself away from the other with whom he had to live, and when he returned to his round, he simply put on the other mask. The human subject does not create a seamless and consistent 'holistic' social world, even in a small-scale milieu such as Todmorden. These are the dialectics of deracinated localism.

So, the latest and greatest are carried around town in heavy bags, but the other aspect of Jean's selling involves the taking of orders. People regularly approach Jean and ask if he can get particular films, CDs or DVDs. Today a man approaches him and asks if he can get a particular season of the TV series *CSI*. Jean says he can, but at this point, the customer reinforces his seriousness, his genuine desire for these DVDs. It seems that Jean has a reputation for occasionally forgetting orders for customers, but then the other aspect of his trade involves drinking in pubs. Some of them 'take the piss a bit', Jean says, when he admits that he has forgotten their discs, but sometimes he simply hasn't been able to locate a torrent for an order yet. Sometimes, if a customer has had a lot to drink, they misunderstand this and assume that he has simply forgotten. Sometimes the customers get edgy, and I saw this once, with a minor stand-off, but Jean says that he hasn't experienced any violence.

Jean prides himself on the quality of his packaging and discs, even if the official artwork is not being directly replicated. He creates what he calls a 'nice package', and after my first couple of days on his rounds, he produced a box set for me, of the 1967 TV series *The Prisoner*. The artwork was unofficial, but professionally done. There is a craft to what Jean does. It is not extremely slick, but he takes great pride in presentation. In Rutter and Bryce's research, CDs and DVDs are by far the most purchased counterfeit goods, closely followed by fashion items, computer games and business software. CDs and DVDs are also purchased most regularly in social spaces such as pubs:

> Rather than being integrated into a subcultural technical elite, the most regular sites of purchase of counterfeit products were more mundane. The most common site for purchasing games was local pubs or social clubs (40% of the total sample), and for purchasing business software school, college or university (28%).

The demographic consumption of CDs tallies with the age range of the 'legitimate' music industry's core market, 21-30 years of age, and this roughly equates with Jean's market for music, although he sells far less CDs these days, mainly DVDs. Rutter and Bryce note the ease with which the latest movies can be downloaded from peer-to peer sites:

> Given the range of content available to internet users at effectively zero cost compared with those available to purchase through established social networks, a rational, economic decision would be primarily to use the internet to obtain counterfeit digital goods. However, our data show that this is not the case, suggesting that purely economic approaches to the purchase of counterfeit goods have limited value in explaining consumption patterns.

Put more simply, people could download their own films and music, but often don't. Jean tells me that the reason he sells in pubs – and sells a lot – is either laziness on behalf of consumers, or intensive working lives. People would rather pay two or three pounds for a DVD in a decent package, than find it, download it, and put it on to a disc for free themselves. If they can do this in the pub over a few pints on Friday, Saturday or Sunday, all the better. Jean then tells me that some people don't have the PC, DVD writer and broadband connection required, essentially, 'the means of production'. Some have these things, but lack the knowledge to complete the process themselves. Rutter and Bryce:

> Although individual motivation may vary, at an aggregate level the decision to purchase counterfeit goods in familiar social environments rather than access them for free online suggests a strong social context and motivation to the consumption of counterfeit goods beyond that gained merely from having ownership or access to the product.

Again, the social context of the exchanges is underlined here. Jean explains how his work in pubs is also a highly social activity. He prides himself on his social network, saying 'I know everyone in this town, and I don't have any enemies.' It also becomes clear that the DVDs themselves have a social function beyond the initial exchange, and I witness a man buying new DVDs from Jean, and then immediately giving two he bought the previous week to a workmate. This seemed to irritate Jean, and a good-natured bit of banter followed, during which Jean somewhat ironically joked about his 'royalties', although when asked about it directly later, he decided that it was 'all fair enough'. Counterfeit DVDs aren't necessarily things to treasure for a lifetime, but their function in social exchanges and to fill leisure time goes beyond this need. Clearly, Jean's products had a wider circulation than one-person-one-view and a wider social function and circulation. This perhaps bolsters the argument that the practice leaks capital away from media producers, but it also underscores its fundamentally social nature.

Jean works to a very tight, regimented timetable, a 'round'. He uses one particular Asian taxi driver for the pubs which have a mile or so of distance between them. He effectively works to rules, some of which are self-imposed, and some imposed upon him by the pub landlords, depending on whether they let him sell on their premises or not. He will slip compliant landlords a few free films, 'porn, sometimes'. He never deals on the street, only in pubs, although he occasionally bends this rule on the street when cars sound their horns to alert him, and pull over. In a place as compact as Todmorden, he is rarely dealing anonymously, if ever, as he could in a city. If he can get into the car for the transaction, he doesn't mind, but occasionally he will put his head into an opened car window, or make the exchange squatting down by the open door, although he is clearly nervous doing so. This often happened on Friday nights.

We go for a break in a pub. Jean tells me that he has long-term ambitions to re-open The Bramsche, a bar named after the German town which Todmorden is twinned with. 'Tod-morden' means 'death-murders' in German, which is a running joke for many Todmorden people, especially when exchange visits take place between residents of Todmorden and Bramsche in Germany, particularly in light of the residency of Doctor Harold Shipman. At this point, The Bramsche has been closed for three years now, metal shutters face out onto the street.

This 'job', for Jean, selling counterfeit DVDs, and he always refers to it as 'my job', or 'work', is a replacement for a 'legitimate' day job which he had to resign from due to internal pressures, and one which will hopefully be recovered, 'legitimised', in Jean's desire to re-open The Bramsche bar. This happens in places such as Todmorden, where flows of capital are weaker than metropolitan centres. In this there is something of a redemption narrative to Jean's practice, in the way he links its ability to generate a profit to his wider hopes and aims, a more mainstream entrepreneurial approach to his practice, which

Rutter and Bryce understand:

> Given the positioning of the purchase of counterfeit goods within everyday leisure and consumption routines and the emerging recognition that consumption is part of other social practices … the purchase of counterfeits seems to share more with an established consumption practice than a subcultural one or a phenomenon explained by criminological perspectives.

Here, I used participant ethnography to try to understand the 'riskiness' of this practice as fully as is ever possible. Jean's mode of address when undertaking transactions was framed in a way which communicated the urgency of the transaction, at the same time as it included some warmth. Occasionally he would have to hurry people along in a slightly more threatening way, again, particularly if lots of drink had been taken. What I realised here was that a mode of address which in most other contexts would have been seen as rude or aggressive was suddenly perfectly normal. I only saw this mode of address by trying to sell myself, and getting it wrong. Getting it 'right' would be to blend in so seamlessly that no-one would see the join, myself included. Because I knew Jean, I had to be placed in this caustic, subjective acid bath, between both our comfort zones, in order for us to see each other.

Attempting to sell DVDs myself had this effect. The landlords didn't know me and gave me very hostile looks. Jean 'squared it' with them, but it placed me in a very real position of criminalization, which an observer can never understand. One pub is frequented by an off-duty policeman. 'Going in cold' may be used to describe taking the plunge into someone else's world, but the experience immediately becomes 'hot': Taking lots of money at once, quickly, when a large group of people crowd around and want to buy several DVDs each, in the knowledge that the police may walk in at any moment, and that this money will remain untaxed, is an entirely different mode of enquiry to observation; feeling the freedom of being no-one's employee, picking your own route and time, drinking on the job, but also feeling the ennui and boredom of a trail of almost empty pubs, and the frisson of violence when customers, who have often had a lot to drink, begin to behave aggressively. All of this is crucial to a researcher's ability to measure the gravity and weightlessness of other lives, but it is still a weakly reflexive practice, ultimately, the researcher can never live there.

This said, Jean and I were of similar ages, from the same place, and had been given roughly the same opportunities, and in this there is something unique about researching the very familiar: Straightforwardly, I could have been him and he could have been me, so very easily, and in this lay the final dialectic of our encounter, the way in which we contained each other.

15

Jean, the busted DVD seller

I'm in Wales, waiting to move north to finish fieldwork, and I get a call from Jean, who tells me he was busted two days ago. He walked into the Golden Lion pub and two police officers appeared from nowhere and started to ask questions. He tells me that his housemate Nicola was in the pub and ran back to the house to clear out a large quantity of incriminating material. He tells me that this was very lucky, and a shrewd move on her part, as he then gave the police access to his house, who confiscated the remaining equipment and resources he needed for his counterfeit DVD operation, thinking they had got everything. He was then taken to Bradford Police station and held without charge for six hours, before being released.

Later, a man from F.A.C.T. – the agency which produced the melodramatic video adverts in the 1990s – came around to visit Jean. The F.A.C.T. official told Jean that he was amazed that he 'wasn't Asian, or selling drugs', alongside DVDs, and that he would probably be 'looking at some community service.' The F.A.C.T. officer's assumptions again underscore Rutter and Bryce's research, and also illuminate a racial dimension to the policing of these activities.

The phone call from Jean explaining what had happened to him coincided with the riots in England, and Jean expressed disgust towards what had happened, telling me that 'there are rules' in society and that the riots were wrong. I spluttered a response without thinking, '…when have you done anything by the rules in the last ten years?!' Jean was genuinely offended by this, in fact, it was really the only time that his easy-going nature broke. He told me to 'fuck off and get some sense': Either I had brought the incongruities between his view of himself as a legitimate entrepreneur and a criminal to the surface, or he didn't see the incongruities at all, in any case, he rang off before the conversation could develop.

I return to interview Jean, in his natural habitat, the pub. Jean is waiting to hear if he will be charged or not, and what with. He has been waiting for four months now, and has heard that it can take up to a year. Jean is now working at The Golden Lion pub, the place where he was arrested, in the kitchen. He is working Monday to Saturday, five hours a day and ten hours on Sunday, making a forty-hour week. I ask how the money is working out in the new job. His ambition to get a mortgage is now effectively gone, even though he has legitimate employment, as his savings are vanishing quickly. He has been granted working tax credit at the highest allowance until next year, when it will be re-assessed. Jean is presented with the un-appetizing prospect of paying tax and national insurance for the first time in a decade. He describes how tight this is, financially, and how he now needs to eat free pub food to make ends meet:

> You eat a meal just when you get there and just before you leave you eat another one, you're not supposed to, but the waitresses get tips and we get fuck all, so... I said [to the chef] any food, we eat it for free...

Again, there seems to be much more autonomy than might be expected in Jean's altering of the rules of employment, and in this his older, entrepreneurial self, in fact his self which sees rules and laws per se only as a hindrance, is still present.

Jean shows me his pay packet, cash in a brown envelope. I ask him about his hours, and he says that 'forty hours a week is a breeze compared to what I used to do.' I ask how many he did when pirating DVDs. 'Eighty, at least', he replies. 'I'd wake up busting for a wee and the machines had to go on first, I'd work 'til midnight putting stuff out...'

'Do you miss it?' I ask. He pauses, before replying, very definitely, 'yeah… the freedom, even though you do more hours, it's whatever you wanna do', and you can stop when you've reached what you need, 'you can work out that… that's enough now, and stop working.' He goes on to explain that he would make up only the current DVD releases to take on his rounds, because the material 'goes out of date very quickly and you always have very limited storage space…' He would bin spare copies, 'fifty or so' which wouldn't sell. He then explains that he could have taken the cases off and re-used them, 'but they were that cheap, it weren't worth it.' (sic).

He talks about giving up smoking and the difficulties of doing this in his working environment. 'You're already in the pub and the beer's free…' 'So you get free beer?' I ask, 'two pints a shift', he replies, 'and you've got fags in your pocket already…' I ask if he carries on drinking after his two free pints, after his shift, and he says 'usually', but he goes somewhere else to do so, after his free beers from work have been consumed. However, I interview him this time in a pub and he refuses a pint of beer, instead drinking orange cordial, as he has a shift later on, and orange cordial is only 40p a pint. The traces of his reduced financial circumstances are all around him.

He talks about his work in the kitchen and his enthusiasm for cooking, he has always cooked quite complex Japanese and Thai meals, as long as I have known him. I ask, 'so are you going to be a chef eventually?' He doesn't answer. After a pause, he says that he will stick it out for a short while, as he wants to 'see it busy' in the kitchen, and talks as though he is an owner or manager of the pub, and claims that he could run the business better than the current manager already. Jean punctuates the conversation a couple of times with speculation about which pubs he could take over, including the Rose and Crown on Halifax Road, which is now derelict. He complains about his boss's lack of calculations on the profit and loss for the meals they serve. His boss told him he is making 75% profit, but Jean claims to have calculated that the whole food operation is losing around £5-800 a month. Jean has lent the landlord 'a grand', which the landlord is paying back in instalments of £150. I ask if he has been repaid the thousand pounds he lent a hard case called Dave earlier and he says 'some of it'.

16

Collapsing the binaries

I began this section by trying to dialectically collapse official and unofficial economies into each other to some extent, and to do the same thing for the concepts of work and non-work. I am adding this to my attempt to do similar things to very binary notions of the urban and rural in the previous chapter. There was a kind of mutant entrepreneurialism to be found in Jean, which often used the language of mainstream small business, sometimes to the extent of making itself blind to its own illegality. But there was also a fugitive quality to be found in much of the 'regular' employment people undertook. It is possible to reach a place where these two facets of working practices become distorted mirror images of each other, and both are framed by the wider practices of capital accumulation.

The eventual capture and near-imprisonment of Jean the DVD pirate led to him getting a 'straight' bar job in the pub where was arrested, after his suspended-sentence was finally issued. When his day in the Crown Court appeared in the local press, the pub he worked in was pictured, illustrating his place of arrest, and he was immediately sacked from his job there. He then became obsessed with this venue, wanting to buy it out, just after he was served with a £100,000 fine he could never pay. There was a psychological attempt to control the uncontrollable, which was heart breaking to observe.

None of this has finally run its course. Recently, the landlord who did the sacking has himself been sacked, and so Jean has managed to re-gain a job right at the heart of his trauma yet again, in the pub he was both arrested in and sacked from, which is owned by Punch, ruthless monopoly capitalists. This pub has seen a revolving door of landlords. Each one came, trying to root himself – and they had all been men up until the current landlady – to find the roots would not hold, despite huge efforts. Jean put up £6,000 to run the pub with three others, talking with great pride of his new status as 'a manager'. Jean's attempt to step into respectability here is also an attempt to step into his own trauma, to control it, which is actually a step into further precariousness. This is a very individual story in some ways, but the key point I want to make here is that the qualities of Jean's existence map onto the experiences of many others in Todmorden who are attempting to 'get by'.

Jean saw the other landlords fail and leave, he knew them all, he gained permission from some of them to sell his pirated goods there, but nonetheless he continues to try to root himself in this instability, as his £100,000 fine hangs over his head. This particular, loaded location – The Golden Lion – the place of his arrest, then the place of his sacking, has become the place he repeatedly tries to tame, to make his own, to root himself in. This is tragic in a deeper, again almost literary sense, although on the ground it has comic, absurd dimensions too. The symbol of the Golden Lion on the English royal coat of arms – and therefore also found in law courts – only bolsters the irony. I accompanied Jean on his day in the county court in Halifax, and watched him look up the symbolism of this heraldry on his iPhone, yet he didn't make the connection. But it is tragic, ultimately: This has become his pathos.

When this is considered, the title 'manager' begins to take on different connotations. What is he attempting to manage here? This man is trying to control the out-of-control nature of his own life, just as Peter and my father try to gain mastery of their own bodies. A week ago as I write, the pub was completely destroyed by flooding and Punch are now selling the shell of a building as a write-off.

Freud explains 'trauma' as a mutant form of anxiety. Anxiety is 'functional' in that it is a form of thinking that attempts to sense future threats and put in place warnings about what might happen. When people are hit suddenly by painful experiences, the opportunity to put anxiety in place is not given, yet there is an attempt to put anxiety in place after the fact, and this is not 'functional', it is trauma.[64] Jean is trying to tame the very space of his trauma.

If the supertanker of capitalism always tries to tame space with approaches to temporality, those thrown overboard, just about bobbing above the waves in its wake, also attempt to do something similar.

All of this has a direct application to Jean, but it can also be applied to the wider landscape: The new middle classes in Todmorden are tentatively moving into the dark of the post-2008 crash situation. They have capital, cultural or otherwise, ego and nous, ingenium, wit, to do the doing. The middle classes are currently re-calibrating their subjectivities, something which often involves taking on the mask of previous forms of working class life, as the 'traditional' working classes – who are in no way traditional in the sense one may get from reading E.P. Thompson, or watching contemporary episodes of Coronation Street – by and large get by with what there is.

Work and non-work can only be viewed dialectically, there are those who are rarely on and those who are rarely off, but there were many more who were always both 'on and off' at all times. I spoke to Adrian, who proclaimed a working class background, but operated as a freelance social entrepreneur – a middle class job – and who often went from Todmorden to Ireland for a single day's work, by train and plane, and 'networked' at all points in between. He seemed to live in Richard Sennett's landscape of normalised anxiety, but he had to an extent come to see and use this as a vehicle, and this is a crucial distinction which Sennett omits between those who are left over from the era of *The Hidden Injuries of Class*[65] and those who live in the new world as though it were natural. But again, the line between the two is anything but neat, as we can see in figures such as Jean, or Peter, who are of the 'old world', but have managed to negotiate the new one through sheer resourcefulness, but often taking much greater risks. The risks the middle classes take on this landscape are less risky, literally, and the difference is their cultural and social capital, which gives them access to the world of doing.

The middle classes are anxious, but their anxiety is attempting to sense an oncoming future, whereas the anxiety encountered in the lower working and underclasses does not often look to the future, it looks inwards, to its own anxieties, and to a past which no longer exists. I felt that most strongly when talking to people such as Michael. His life was totally legitimate, he lived as 'a citizen', but he experienced nothing but precariousness. Of course, it could be argued that attempting to sense an oncoming future – as figures such as Adrian did, with their 'always on' practices of networking, is just as dysfunctional as staring backwards into a dead past, but the qualities of the lives lived under these two related yet vastly different psychological and temporal attitudes are polar, they are the dialectical flipsides of one another. Those undertaking work in informal economies provided a negative mirror image of the supposedly 'respectable' economies. They were trying to make themselves respectable via this work, which was often almost impossible, but then this also seemed to apply to many workers paying tax and national insurance.

In the example of Jean we have proof that Mario Candeias is correct to state that precarité is a phenomena which affects both the 'precariat' and the 'cyberteriat', but in Jean we see both these paradigms in one figure: the technologically competent, and the black marketeer and the precarious inhabitant of an underground economy. Because of this, we need to be careful with excessively neat, binary explanations, imposed from above on vast swathes of social life. In this, I am advocating a kind of micro-Marxism, to nuance the persistent macro-Marxism of writers such Candeias. But Candeias is far from wrong, to be clear, particularly when he states that precarité saturates all forms of social life, and here again, the excessively neat binaries begin to dissolve. Precarité does saturate all forms of life because they all live under a capitalist system of distribution, but dissolving the binaries in this way should never dissolve the political project of railing against the starkly unequal qualities of lives lived in a single landscape. What also comes across very clearly though, is that this railing, for those who we are concerned, is often directed towards the other, and not at any wider system or state.

The points I am making here relate to the craft of qualitative community ethnography: The dialectic is in the detail. It is possible to simplistically find people who are working or not working. We can do this statistically, as Fenton and Dermott did: In Todmorden, of those people registered by the state, we have 47% 'professional' workers, 37% skilled and semi-skilled manual workers, and 16% on benefits. Of course, 'on and off' describes a binary switch, but 'on and off' also describes a *single state* which saturates lived experience in places such as Todmorden. We have to go there and live in it to see this, we cannot just announce the situation from above. The statistics are Raymond Williams's ice cube tray,[66] but 'on and off', as a qualitative experience, is what I have chased in Todmorden, and I found the best explanation of that in perhaps its most extreme examples.

Rough statistical breakdowns such as these are useful, but it is much more accurate to locate and add to this picture the work which is not worth doing, or barely worth doing, or just about worth doing, as well as those operating outside the official economies. To make distinctions such as these, rather than simple statements about who is 'in' or 'out' of work is a much more ethical practice, because as we can see, if we hold to the experience of work, suddenly, the in-or-out, legitimate-or-not binaries are emptied of meaning. At worst, they simply reproduce the epistemologies of the law and 'justice', when we should hold to an ethical position which tries to produce itself from outside of these frameworks, as much as that is ever possible. In this sense, again, I am making a case for a kind of anarchist form of craft for community researchers.[67]

All the people I have introduced briefly here provided an incredible example of attempting to root in rootlessness. Their 'deracinated localism' was perhaps the most extreme, but it mapped onto the deracinated localisms of all the other groups I encountered in Todmorden. I want to turn to some of those groups now, in order to further explore the dialectics of deracinated localism.

17

Not local and totally local, the organic and inorganic, pure and impure

Again, to continue my dialectical thread, the themes which carry over here, from my last chapter, are work and non-work. But here the dialectic begins to take us through the politics of voluntarism, into the middle class social world of Todmorden. Working for free, or work which is 'not worth doing', or 'barely worth doing', is re-cast in a different hierarchical order here: Once in this class, voluntary labour becomes 'cultural capital'. I left Jean in the last chapter, eventually he found a job as a cook in one of the moorland pubs, working as an untrained chef for minimum wage, reliant on Working Tax Credit to get by. But there is another side to food culture in Todmorden, and that is the increasing number of 'organic' outlets and growing campaigns.

As I have already explained, Todmorden is much like many other 'market towns', when assessed both statistically and culturally, but it differs in several key ways, and one of these key differences involves its local food growing group, Incredible Edible Todmorden (IET) and other 'localist' ventures. IET 'grow and campaign for local food', but they differ from many other 'localised' groups, undertaking similar projects all across the country, in that they are exceptionally effective at projecting themselves via national and global media. In fact, whenever someone told me 'Todmorden was on the telly this week' during fieldwork, I could nearly always guess correctly that IET were involved. During the period of 2010-2012, IET became as ubiquitous a symbol of Todmorden in the national media as the Stoodley Pike monument is locally. IET's stated aims and ambitions are well summarised by Julie Guthman, when she describes the characteristics of many American alternative food groups, who value 'real, organic food, putting one's hands in the soil, and knowing where one's food comes by shopping at local and alternative venues.'[68]

I explored IET through ethnography and public discourses, partly because a large part of the project is public or media discourses, but partly because some of the key players proved to be recalcitrant interviewees. In fact, the one person who agreed to be formally interviewed also turned out to be a less than enthusiastic participant.

18

Polythene tunnels and powertools

Nick Brown of IET seemed un-cooperative at first. I met him in one of two large polytunnel greenhouses at the Walsden growing site. Nick Brown looks like a hippy, bearded, with big sideburns, lots of hair, and a beaten-up hat. A similar-looking volunteer with a dog was present, working on the site. He seemed to be preparing wood to make beds for planting. It was raining. Firstly, Nick claimed not to remember me asking to come over and speak to him, despite agreeing by email to an interview only two days previously. He carried on drilling and using powertools as I spoke, seemingly deliberately. He was standoffish to such a degree, initially, that I experienced a moment where the dialogue could have continued, or I could have walked out. He asked me who I had spoken to in IET. I told him that I had emailed Pam Warhurst, Mary Clear – two key IET players – and himself. 'But who have you spoken to', he asked, as though I were seven years old. Pam, Mary and himself, I repeated. 'You're great at not answering questions aren't you?' he said, in a manner which was half-joking, half-hostile, but mainly patronising. 'You're interviewing me!' I exclaimed. 'Yes' he replied.

Then he warmed slightly, but only slightly. That level of bombast is, I imagine, quite hard to maintain face-to-face. He began to use a slightly more reasonable tone, but he continued to intersperse this with frequent bouts of powertool use. Often, when I started speaking, he would drill a hole, wiping out my speech, then he would stop and ask me to 'carry on.' The cassette sounds like a rehearsal for a comedy sketch. Firstly, I asked Nick Brown how the site began. He told me that:

Pam [Warhurst] went to Riggs and said "give us some land".

Riggs said "there's some land do something with it." So, we looked at it – or rather I looked at it – and thought OK we could do a nice community thing and have a shared community garden and allotments... everybody'd have somewhere to grow and they might talk to each other about vegetables... but what would probably happen is a load of 50-somethings would come and colonise it and say "get orf my land", that's your bit, that's my bit, boundaries...

Pam Warhurst, along with Mary Clear, are two founders of IET. Warhurst has run Bear Wholefoods in Todmorden for many years, an original co-op with a Victorian frontage, which now sells organic food from a shop downstairs and a café on the first floor. I was surprised by Nick's admission about the initial idea to provide allotments, which was then decided against, and I wanted to check it: 'So the 50-somethings coming in didn't happen because you thought it would get taken over by the 50-somethings?' I asked, just to make sure I had heard correctly. He then powertooled again, possibly because he didn't want to answer the question immediately. After a long stretch of white noise, he replied:

Rather than do that, what we decided to do was build a training centre and get young people involved with growing and teach people how to do it, because nobody knows how to do this stuff anymore, and we didn't really think that if we had a bunch of people with allotments that would necessarily happen.

This seemed like a steep claim in the face of the recent revival of allotment culture in Britain.[69] Waiting lists nationally have multiplied. Nick then explained that IET had decided to try to set up 'a model business with the intention of seeing if it's possible to make some kind of living by growing stuff... and finding out how to do it, finding out how to do the business stuff, so that we can then take on apprentices', so that they can set up businesses of their own in turn.

This came as something of a surprise to me, as in Todmorden town centre, and in the national and international media messages which IET circulates, the explanation of their project always rests on the vegetable beds in town where people can pick organic fruit and vegetables for free, what IET call their 'propoganda gardens'. Essentially, Green explained an 'alternative' small business model to me, for organic, local, sustainable growing.

Later, I came across the idea that projects such as these don't necessarily create alternatives, but essentially reproduce neoliberalism at a local scale. For instance, Born and Purcell[70] argue against claims that local systems produce better sustainability or justice than production at other, larger scales. The agendas themselves, they say, are what create the qualitative aspects of the systems, not the scales themselves. They argue that 'it is critical to avoid the local trap.' Roberto Sonnino backs this up, by stating that '…re-scaling food activities does not necessarily provide a solution to the lack of social justice in the contemporary food system.' However, she tackles this 'local trap' argument by debating that the local can in fact create sustainable food production, but that it also can and in fact does reproduce neoliberalism within its local scale. We are, she says, always thrown back on the ideologies of 'consumerism and choice'.[71]

This idea, that 'local' projects which are concerned with notions of justice and 'food security' reproduce neoliberalism, seemed to be immediately present in the interview with Nick, who went on to explain that 'one of the challenges we face is how to make this sustainable financially.' One response to this, according to Nick, is to set up courses to teach people how to grow organically. The usual horticulture courses are 'under-subscribed', he told me, but he thinks that the 'organic' curriculum might take off and become bigger, and someone is currently establishing new syllabuses. Agricultural practices 'based on oil' made the larger local concerns end, Nick says, but he thinks that it's possible to make a living from a site such as this one, 'it's not a full living yet, but it could become one', he said. Every time one of Nick's powertools erased the conversation, I wondered where the power was coming from, after this comment about oil-based endeavours. I was also interested to know who owned the land, and Nick told me that it still belongs to Gordon Rigg, the garden centre: 'They are the leaseholder, but it's a free lease'.

'It's almost like feudalism', I said, without thinking. Nick recoiled. 'How is that like feudalism?' he asked, witheringly. 'Peppercorn rents, to landlords... to do stuff...' I replied. Nick snapped back, 'under a feudal system you had to work a certain amount of days for the landlord, so it wasn't free.' A long blast of white noise followed, as he chainsawed another plank.

Later, Nick told me that the biggest source of labour on this site comes from the Calderdale Community Service programmes, one day per week. This means that unpaid workers are sourced from a pool of people who have been convicted of crimes, but whose sentences are community labour. Of course, this isn't feudalism, Nick was right, but my perhaps thoughtless comment acted as a kind of 'provo' moment, illuminating some of the ideological paradoxes under projects such as this one. Later, it struck me that there may be some parallels to draw here, that the new peasantry may actually be an underclass who face the criminal justice system, and who are being fed into projects such as this. This without mentioning the fact that autonomous growing was dismissed without an experiment to see how it might develop.

Of course, these are speculative points, but what struck me very clearly here, as the interview unfolded, was how all the 'purity' of the project was explained in terms of their particular vision of the 'organic', and a way of 'saving' the locals who 'know no better'. The 'purity' of the system of labour and money, power and justice, underpinning this state of affairs, perceived or otherwise, remained un-examined.

The assumptions which were being made turned out to have quite particular, classed dimensions as well. At one point, Nick talked about expanding the message about food security beyond the 'five per cent of middle classes' who 'get it'. 'You're not finding any worried working classes then?' I asked. 'Yeah, we are', he said, 'but it's slowly slowly with them... here's a bit of nice voluntary work, which is nice to do... which is fun'. Don't give them any heavy messages, he explained. 'So the middle classes get it?' I asked. 'The middle classes do', he replied, adding, 'well some of them do, but some of them just want to put their heads in the sand...'

Nick is unpaid at the moment, and works at the site full-time, as is Michael, who also works virtually full-time on the site. Michael wasn't present on the day I visited, but the IET 'insiders' are aiming for this to pay them wages eventually: They are engaged in an act of providing themselves with future employment; in this it relies on the unpaid voluntary labour of others. This is linked to making the site financially viable, and they have just started to sell produce to The Rake, a Tapas restaurant in nearby Littleborough, and The Staff of Life in Todmorden. Both are 'gastropubs', and both are classed in a different order to The Golden Lion and The Shepherds Rest, which are the locations of Jean's trials and tribulations, past and present. The places which take on local produce – such as The Bramsche – are often also freehold, whereas The Golden Lion was owned by the monopoly capitalists Punch, so there is a wider politics of ownership which produces this essentially classed landscape. There is a further politics of ownership in Nick Brown's ability to run the IET Walsden growing site: he bought a large ex-industrial property in town for his business, but was then forced to wind his business down, and now he rents the space to artists, so as a landlord he is free 'to do interesting stuff.' Michael's wife works, and he looks after the baby, and the baby comes to work with him every day.

Nick then explained that IET wanted to engage people in a fun way. He told me about the 'sustainable towns movement', who engage with people via 'fear'. He told me that 'they think the world is gonna end… and we think the world is gonna end…' He trailed off at this point, but after a pause, he explained that his personal concern was with food security. He then told me about another group, who, to him, are the flipside to the sustainable towns movement: 'Permaculture enthusiasts', he told me, are a 'bit religious'. You can't just 'save the planet', you have to 'love the planet and all that'. This movement, he explained, is mixed in with new age spirituality. Nick told me that if you have to accept a religion or 'something which feels like a religion' – even though he 'agrees with a lot of what they say' – he feels that their message is essentially 'unpalatable.'

There was a kind of augury under Nick's admission that IET also think 'the world is gonna end', which nonetheless accused others of disingenuous forms of augury. An essentially Christian set of discourses could be detected at the back of his monologue, which nonetheless set itself against religious dogma. There was a way in which Nick placed his own latent messianism very clearly against other forms of messianism. We seemed at this point, to be back at the different, competing non-conformisms of the early nineteenth century. Nietzsche called these traces of religion, operating under a secularised social surface, the 'shadow of god'. I was reminded strongly of the different sects of Methodism in this area when talking to Nick – accounted for by E.P. Thompson during his time in the region.[72]

I want to leave Nick Brown in his polytunnel for a little while now, to explore the ways in which the core arguments coming from Nick – and their ghosts – could also be chased onto the public and media discourses which IET create.

19

Spreading the good news, some public and media discourses

IET were represented by their co-founder, Pam Warhurst, on the *Radio 4* current affairs programme *You and Yours*, in December, 2011. The group had recently announced that it aimed to make Todmorden 'self-sufficient' in food by 2018. The *Daily Mail* covered the IET story earlier in the year. In their article, IET co-founder Mary Clear explained: 'It's a very ambitious aim. But if you don't aim high, you might as well stay in bed, mightn't you?'[73]

The *Radio 4 You and Yours* presenter asked Warhurst how 'hundreds' of volunteers were going to grow for a population of around 16,000. Warhurst readily admitted that her stated goal was unlikely to ever be fully achieved. Her stock response to tricky questions like these seemed to be that IET were currently undertaking a phase which was focussed on changing attitudes, essentially doctoring local ideologies. Warhurst wanted everyone in Todmorden to 'live in an edible landscape.'

She described what she called the 'propaganda gardens' in Todmorden, essentially small plots in town where people can uproot and take vegetables for free, and how everybody is 'getting the bug', becoming excited, and getting involved. David Harvey talks of how 'mental conceptions of everyday life' need to change, along with all the other elements, technological, economic, in order to revolutionise production and society.[74] This, it seems, is what IET were undertaking in their initial phase. Warhurst then described the 'yes we can' of localised food production. The use of Obama's phrase seemed to compare IETs efforts with the need to revive whole countries after the crash of 2008. Warhurst explained her desire for young people to 'stay in our town and get a job in our town.' Again, her rhetoric seemed to attach itself to wider, national issues, as well as local ones, when it suited. IETs ambitions do not end with steep production quotas, but move into the wider local discourses of youth unemployment, and community more generally, rhetorically at least:

> Incredible Edible is also about much more than plots of veg. It's about educating people about food, and stimulating the local economy. There are lessons in pickling and preserving fruits, courses on bread-making, and the local college is to offer a BTEC in horticulture. The thinking is that young people who have grown up among the street veg. may make a career in food.[75]

There is a well-meaning assumption that the 'youth problem' will be solved by IET. To return to the *Daily Mail* article:

> Jenny Coleman, 62, who retired here from London, explains: "We need something for our young people to do. If you're an 18-year-old, there's got to be a good answer to the question: why would I want to stay in Todmorden?" [76]

What emerges here though, as a solution, is a mix of voluntarism and small-scale capitalism:

> Crucially, the scheme is also about helping local businesses. The Bear, a wonderful shop and cafe with a magnificent original Victorian frontage, sources all its ingredients from farmers within a 30-mile radius. There's a brilliant daily market. People here can eat well on local produce, and thousands now do. Meanwhile, the local school was recently awarded a £500,000 Lottery grant to set up a fish farm in order to provide food for the locals and to teach useful skills to young people.

It is perhaps even more crucial to point out here that The Bear, the 'wonderful shop and cafe with a magnificent original Victorian frontage', is owned and run by the IET founder Pam Warhurst. The *Daily Mail* also covers what they see as Todmorden's human geography in relation to some of these questions:

> 'If you're assuming it's largely peopled by middle-class grand-mothers, think again. Nor is this place a mecca for the gin-and-Jag golf club set. A third of households do not own a car; a fifth do not have central heating…'

Yet in the following sentence, Vincent Graff, the *Mail* journalist, states that 'You can snap up a terrace house for £50,000 – or spend close to £1 million on a handsome stone villa with seven bedrooms.' Owen Jones[77] explains how the assumptions of high-level journalists distort their reportage, essentially using their own well-paid lives as an assumed conceptual floor for their polemics. It is perhaps pointless to try to find veracity in *Daily Mail* journalism, but it is important to point out that the 'humbleness' of the town outlined in this article jars somewhat with the assumption that £50,000 is somehow cheap. The house price and rent freeze-out of Hebden Bridge locals has been covered by Darren Smith's research, in relation to gentrification, as well as what he calls 'greentrification':

> …the revitalization of the Hebden Bridge district has not taken place without significant social cost and upset. The influx of relatively affluent in-migrants has been accompanied by house price inflation, substantially higher than the regional trend. Subsequently, the relatively less affluent indigenous households have been displaced from the location or margin-alized to the less desirable parts of the location… The "processes of revitalization" must minimize the detrimental effect on the indigenous inhabitants. [78]

Todmorden's house prices have not increased in the way Hebden Bridge's have, at least not yet, although many of the voices coming from my ethnography assume 'that "green" lot', as one man described them to me, were pushing house prices beyond affordability. At the time I began to undertake my fieldwork, house prices in Todmorden had frozen and were declining slightly, yet these assumptions continued well into 2012. Culturally, on the ground, one could be forgiven for thinking that unemployment was not the main problem, but middle class incomers.

However, the pronounced split between these working class voices, who relied on employment and seemed frustrated, and the IET insiders, was very real, as Nick Brown intimated. The working classes nearly always explained their lives as essentially imposed upon from outside, but the middle class 'greens' seemed to 'get on' and run projects with some autonomy, gaining Lottery grants, and other forms of funding. This is also reflected in the self-reliance narrative in the *Daily Mail* article, which grates noisily against the sides of gentrification research coming from people such as Darren Smith. The *Daily Mail* article describes Joe Strachan:

...a wealthy U.S. former sales director who decided to settle in Tod with his Scottish wife, after many years in California. He is 61 but looks 41. He became active with Incredible Edible six months ago, and couldn't be happier digging, sowing and juicing fruit. I find myself next to him, sheltering from the driving rain. Why, I ask, would someone forsake the sunshine of California for all this? His answer sums up what the people around here have achieved. "There's a nobility to growing food and allowing people to share it. There's a feeling we're doing something significant rather than just moaning that the state can't take care of us. Maybe we all need to learn to take care of ourselves."[79]

Operating under this quote is an ideology which does not suggest a local buttressing for a welfare state now under attack, but a new rhetoric of essentially Tory self-reliance, which uses the language and actions of 1970s countercultures in the service of its own, and is in fact rooted further back, locally and historically, in Co-operative ideologies. Paul Barker explains how this area of the valley had thriving Co-ops, but little trade union militancy; Heywood, Heywood and Jennings and Law back this up in relation to Todmorden.[80]

Of course, the inherent conservatism in this quote is undoubtedly why the *Daily Mail* singled this voice out from some of the others, but the self-reliance narrative was reproduced by Nick Brown in interview, and by Pam Warhurst and others in IET media discourses. The politics of voluntarism are the most glaring issues. How is the 'nobility' of free labour and 'sharing' underpinned by other activities, in this case a successful life spent in mainstream American capitalism? These wider questions are perhaps beyond the scope of this book, mainly because IET is a relatively new project, but those questions will inevitably writhe under this book, as long as the political and economic landscape shifts in response to the crashes of 2008, and the continuing crisis in the eurozone.

But what I want to concentrate on here are the complex meshes of cultural assumptions which underpin these discourses, in relation to my theme of deracinated localism. Because it is clear that in IETs rhetoric, there is an attempt to 'root themselves' – quite literally – in local soil, at the same time as contested narratives about the 'un-local' continue around super-marketization, unemployment and migration, which I want to deal with in turn. As we can see, in IETs hands, these debates are shot through with distinction and nostalgia, and I want to focus in further on some of those aspects now.

20

Class, distinction and nostalgia

Underneath the kind of rhetoric IET broadcast, is a Bourdieusian cultural capital question: who gets to work for free for IET, and how. How is the cultural hierarchy of the project distributed? There are a set of assumptions encoded into IETs rhetoric which can be teased out, in order to begin to try to answer some of these bigger questions.

For instance, on *You and Yours*, Pam Warhurst claimed that there are wider cultural problems for IET to overcome, that 'we've lost the skills', for instance the ability to pickle for winter. In this, she repeated much of what Nick Brown said to me when I interviewed him. There was some nostalgia here, in Warhurst's look back to 'old crafts', but there was also a racial and cultural dimension: Pickling and making chutney are not exclusively white Western food preservation practices, but this was an appeal to a very English dimension of allotment-type growing and seasonal work. There is a classed dimension too, *Radio 4* is perceived to be middle class, the presenters often joke about '*Radio 4* audiences' as 'intelligent listeners', and many of the items on You and Yours contain unexamined nostalgias. Warhurst was probably just playing to those expectations, but the tip of a sense of othering emerged in her monologue, which Dr. Roberta Sonnino of Cardiff University – the other guest on this section of You and Yours – seemed to pick up on.[81] Sonnino, as an academic, has published much research on localism and food production. On You and Yours she spoke about cultural diversity, ethnic diversity, and the importance of food production being accessible to everybody. She spoke of moving away from a 'parochial or defensive' view of localism, and into a flexible or open-ended take on localism. She didn't see any problems with IETs project, but only if they were undertaking flexible, opened-out cultural practices, but she was effectively cut off when the show ran out of time. I switched the radio off and began to fill the silence by speculating on what Sonnino may have said about cultural and ethnic diversity, about food production being accessible to everybody, and what this might mean for IET and Todmorden communities more generally.

I then began to research the subject more widely, and found that my concerns were partly addressed by Sonnino's written research, and that of Julie Guthman, who describes how in the United States, 'under the banner of food justice', many programmes try to bring 'good food' to African-Americans via 'a set of discourses that reflect whitened cultural histories, such as the value of putting one's hands in the soil.'[82] I would add that here in Todmorden this is implicitly rural, anti-urban, and classed. Guthman describes how 'the African Americans who are the target of these efforts appear to reject them', which 'in some sense replicates the very phenomenon being addressed – the effect of white desire to enroll black people in a particular set of food practices.' In Todmorden, this 'rejection' is a white working class one. I spoke to Adrian Ashton, a local social entrepreneur and Christian, who explained, with some sadness, how 'local people' refused to get involved with IETs project. Adrian has worked with IET and makes his living trying to connect different community groups and projects. I also experienced a great deal of white working class resentment towards IET, but also a lot of ambivalence, which actually seemed to be no less powerful in its resistance.

There was very little of the detail I am providing here in those narratives – why would there be – but the refusal was nonetheless tangible, and that refusal was deployed in lines such as: 'like I've got the time to plant stuff for nowt' (nothing) [Gary] to the more blunt 'nobody works for free' [Dave] and the more culturally resentful comments about 'bloody 'ippies' which I heard a few times, and which echoed Jeanette Edwards' work on nearby Bacup.[83]

Guthman points out 'the race-inflected, even missionary, aspects of alternative food politics', which occur 'despite the pretense of color-blindness.' I want to argue here that IET don't get as far as pretending to be class or colour neutral, but that their own class make-up and missionary framing can be detected very strongly on the surface of their rhetoric. Guthman speaks of her own students, entering the course she teaches, with a kind of white missionary zeal, stating that 'whitened cultural histories are what animate my students [and] how many of these projects reflect white desires and missionary practices.' Guthman describes the wide-eyed, 'if only people knew' tendency in her students, who turn up with romanticised, often pre-modern concepts of alternative food production.[84]

Guthman outlines the pre-constructed nature of these discourses, explaining that 'the types of projects that excite' students 'do not emerge out of thin air'. She adds that '...current arenas of activism around food and agriculture already reflect a delimited politics of the possible.' I would argue that IETs canniness as a media player is creating a delimited set of assumptions about the possible as it progresses, as well as concealing most of its agency. Also, if one exchanges what Guthman has said about racialised cheap labour here for free labour, some of which is sourced from pools of people one step away from prison, there is some traffic. The IET labour is racialised – it is largely white – and the project is reproducing a classed, Victorian missionary rhetoric, which has a locus in some of its heritage, for instance the frontage of Bear Wholefoods, Pam Warhurst's domain, is also an original Co-op.

Guthman talks about how alternative food projects are 'coded white'. I agree, but I would like to render the discourses even more complex, by arguing that they are coded white and middle class, and gendered female or 'feminine' from within. This though, again, is something which remains in the air with their media messages, as going to speak to Nick Brown provided a gruff, masculine counterpoint to these claims. Nonetheless, IETs rhetoric assimilates a kind of flattened countercultural discourse, almost to the point of 'New Age' mysticism, at the same time as some of its 'insiders' distance themselves from these aspects. This ties in with Guthman's insights into her students and their interests in pre-modern farming, which are central to IETs discourses. Guthman describes '...the horticultural therapy movement, which has popularised the notion that direct contact with nature in gardening and farming provides a path towards healing and empowerment.'[85] This is reflected in some of Hazel Southam's descriptions, for her article on IET in *Geographical* magazine. She writes that: 'Teenagers on their way to school are picking peas and popping them from pod to mouth instead of buying sweets.' Southam also interviews an IET volunteer who tells her: '"My grandchildren pick pea pods on the way to school", she continues. "I think it's really good. It's brilliant." And then she hugs me. Twice.' This rhetoric of giving is employed in a very specific, cosy way, and it is often gendered. The *Daily Mail* journalist asked:

> So what's to stop me turning up with a huge carrier bag and grabbing all the rosemary in the town? "Nothing," says Mary. What's to stop me nabbing all the apples? "Nothing." All your raspberries? "Nothing." It just doesn't happen like that, she says. "We trust people. We truly believe — we are witness to it — that people are decent." When she sees the Big Issue seller gathering fruit for his lunch, she feels only pleasure. What does it matter, argues Mary, if once in a while she turns up with her margarine tub to find that all the strawberries are gone? "This is a revolution," she says. "But we are gentle revolutionaries. Everything we do is underpinned by kindness." The idea came about after she and co-founder Pam

Warhurst, the former owner of the town's Bear Cafe, began fretting about the state of the world and wondered what they could do. They reasoned that all they could do is start locally, so they got a group of people, mostly women, together in the cafe. ... "Wars come about by men having drinks in bars, good things come about when women drink coffee together," says Mary. "Our thinking was: there's so much blame in the world — blame local government, blame politicians, blame bankers, blame technology — we thought, let's just do something positive instead."

Online, the article is filed in the 'Femail' section, although this 'kindness' is also more generally and fuzzily put down to Todmorden's small social world:The day I visit, the town is battered by a bitterly-cold rain storm. Yet the place radiates warmth. People speak to each other in the street, wave as neighbours drive past, smile. If the phrase hadn't been hijacked, the words "we're all in this together" would spring to mind.[86]

Again, there is little point taking tabloid coverage at face value, but these assumptions about a benign because small-scale social world are interesting, and do not stay inside the Daily Mail's pages, they can be found in the town, being employed sociologically, in different ways. There is a further link here to the mythical idea that small scale production is synonymous with justice and purity. These claims of an almost messianic effect, radiating from the IET project, do not limit themselves to a general 'hippy' friendliness. IET even claim to be combating crime by planting vegetables. Hazel Southam's Geographical magazine article describes the fruit trees outside the police station, before attributing a drop in crime to Incredible Edible's activities: The police report that vandalism is down since the planting of the IET vegetables. Sergeant Michael Bowden claims that 'Crime has gone down because everyone has ownership of the land.' The vandalism figures have dropped slightly, but the latter statement regarding land ownership is fundamentally erroneous. Warhurst says:

> If you take a grass verge that was used as a litter bin and a dog toilet and turn it into a place full of herbs and fruit trees, people won't vandalise it. I think we are hard-wired not to damage food.

IETs 'link' with the crime has a further dimension. I asked Nick Brown about the Community Service programmes at one point. He told me:

> we don't get sent people who have got... serious violence, mostly we get people who've been growing dope and there are lots and lots of them...

I agreed with this and pointed out how many prosecutions I had seen in the Todmorden News over the last few years. Nick told me that the 'Police turned a blind eye to it for several years and then they got a new Chief Superintendent.'

In late December, the Todmorden News front page trumpeted the donation of horticultural equipment, recently confiscated from local cannabis producers, to Todmorden High School:

> Inspector Dave Browning, of the Upper Valley Neighbourhood Policing Team (NPT) believes some of this equipment can be used for the public benefit by making its available to community groups. In recent years Todmorden has developed several gardening and growing schemes, spearheaded by Incredible Edible Todmorden, and under the guidance of teacher Paul Murray the High School has devoted a lot of time, work, funds and space to developing gardens at the Ewood Lane site, produce finding its way onto the school's menus via head chef Tony Mulgrew and his team. Canes,

composting plant pots and water butts are expensive to buy, and accordingly re-using the confiscated items will save the school cash. Inspector Browning said: "This was a great opportunity to create another positive out of closing a cannabis farm in our community, and I am delighted that the school are able to put the items to good use. Once we have sent all the plants at a cannabis farm to be destroyed, we regularly donate any equipment which can be re-used to local community groups."

The comments on the Todmorden News website were all pro-cannabis, apart from one which rather apologetically sided with the police. The productive power of cannabis growers in Todmorden and its immediate locality is clear, even if one only takes a six month slice of police raids:

21 Aug 2011: A man found with cannabis plants in his cellar has been told he will work in the community as his punishment... 6 Jan 2012: Drugs were seized in a New Year's Eve raid... they found 130 suspected cannabis plants inside... 14 Jan 2012: A father and son have been accused of growing £14000 worth of cannabis... 31 Jan 2012: '£25k cannabis 'bunker' was found...

And on it goes. Locally, 'to do a grow' or 'be involved with the green' also means to cultivate marijuana as a cash crop indoors using hydroponic technology. There may be little more to make out of this point than cheap irony, but I do think it is an irony which has some mileage. These reports of raids on cannabis producers show that the practice is not small-scale in the valley. There is a very clear line between those who are assumed to be 'legitimate' independent and local horticultural producers, and it is clear in this case, because the line is drawn by the law.[87]

Yet this line became a little fuzzier when I discovered that, prior to the visit of HRH Prince Charles – a fan of IET – Network Rail were oblivious to Incredible Edible planting on their land. There is perhaps a different scale of illegality here, but in light of such admissions, there is also a moral and moralizing dimension to the Todmorden News front page about the donation of horticultural equipment from cannabis farming raids. In this sense the project can demarcate itself using language as its 'law', broadcast through powerful media networks. The IET rhetoric is very powerful, hooked-up, as it is, to similarly powerful national debates around green cultures, sustainability and local horticulture. The wider, national 'Big Society' debates emerging from the coalition government at the time also sat comfortably and conveniently over this kind of local rhetoric, like a kind of protecting umbrella. A picture of who gets to do what kind of illegal growing and where begins to emerge in traces such as the Network Rail plots, and a set of essentially provincial cultural assumptions begin to emerge.

IET have since been given official permission by the council to plant on council land.

When I spoke to her, Mary Clear indulged in a little radical posturing over their own disregard for planning laws or legality. She explained how they were supposed to get planning permission for the local green route, but they hadn't bothered, and had continued unchallenged. 'Just do it', she told me, 'the prisons are full in this country and I'd like a rest.' She told me that the town council have virtually no powers, and in any case there is now a profound lack of council workers to police what they do. Under this, it seemed that if planning was ignored under the alibi of this powerful, rusticated rhetoric, it was fine. Clear talked of planting free vegetables at the Health Centre, initially without permission. Yet Todmorden's relatively new Health Centre is a PFI building, and so IETs growing on the site literally sits on wider neoliberal finance capital and infrastructure.

These are the real assemblages of meaning which researchers

need to access, underneath the gloss of Clear's rhetoric.

Of course, again, we have to be careful to demarcate what IET says about itself, and what others say about it. For instance, Hazel Southam was not shy about taking her own provincialism further, in order to make a lightweight nationalist joke in her article: 'The EU has given Pam a grant of £20,000 to train would-be Tom and Barbara Goods from mainland Europe over the next two years. No-one mentions the delicious irony of teaching the French a thing or two about food.' Southam wrote for the Telegraph for ten years, so again, we should not be too surprised, but this kind of rhetoric is interesting. Her throwaway, mildly toxic line actually contains its own antidote, in the reference to the EU grant, at the same time as it seems implicitly eurosceptic.

But the inherent contradictions don't necessarily stop her rhetoric from being powerfully affective. There is a particular kind of Englishness being broadcast through these connotations, produced at moments like this, and whether intended by IET insiders or not, a particular view of their project, and of the town more widely, is being produced through these rhetorical assemblages, and it is these rhetorical assemblages that I am largely concerned with here.

I attended an IET tour which began from the Unitarian church, where Mary Clear gave a Powerpoint presentation. This contained an illustration which took the form of a Borromean knot of holistic spiritualism, describing IETs mission as 'earth care, from cradle to cradle'. Yet when she talked about Hebden Bridge, the 'holism' broke down as she described the split of retail outlets there as 'dirty shops for dirty people and groovy shops for groovy people.' The classed disgust was right on the surface. I spoke to Clear afterwards, and she told me that 'working class people cause all the damage in Tod, and because of us there is now no environmental crime.' I mentioned the violence in town at weekends, and she told me that 'if you don't look like a dope head or piss head you will get attacked.' I told her that I was attacked a year previously, and they responded by saying that I 'probably looked too middle class.' I then explained that I was from a working class background.

This class split maps onto those who engage with IETs project, Clear told me that 'Guardian readers come to us, another group does not...' The classed rhetoric also extended to food practices, 'people don't know how to cook', Clear told me, 'the ping of the microwave rules the country.' She then described a recent visit to the Royal Society of the Arts, 'the Creme de la Creme, and it's a right middle class do, but Pam [Warhurst] went in to ask for a green corridor across the country.' She also told me that when the IET supporter Prince Charles visited, he had told her, 'Mary, when I'm King, you can have as much land as you want.'

Clear also claimed to be 'totally surprised' by all the attention IET generated, 'it's weird', she says, 'we have never issued a press release'. Here was an alibi, as they were running a powerful propaganda machine; websites and Twitter feeds, which don't require press releases in the traditional sense. Clear also claimed that 'there is no empire' of IET, and yet community allotments were disregarded out of hand, as Nick Brown told me. Again, this is the realpolitik under the gloss.

21

The politics of labour and the land

I want to return briefly to dialectical thinking here, because there are many misleading binaries, which are presented as straightforwardly intelligible by IET.

IET literally proclaim themselves to be 'totally local', indeed part of their campaign is called 'Totally Locally', and this can be seen on bumper stickers up and down the valley. Yet IET often add un-local elements to their rhetoric, occasionally dipping into national debates, for instance around youth unemployment, in order to add gravitas to their ideologies. In some ways this is understandable, as they are responding to national and international debates around scarcity and ecological crises, and their response to that is to localise in order to reduce those problems.

Yet in many ways this narrative conceals almost as much as it provides, as should hopefully be clear by now. The labour IET sources is local, but it is also unpaid, and so the capital which that labour uses to reproduce itself on a daily basis must come from wider national and global circuits. Some of this labour is also essentially forced, through criminal justice system work programmes. The capital IET uses for infrastructure and resources has come mainly from National Lottery funds, and so again, it is being taken from wider national circuits, which are also classed in particular ways. IET has gained donations, 'locally', from Gordon Rigg nurseries, including land and equipment. But Gordon Rigg sources its goods internationally, and therefore its capital flows from the surplus labour carried out on global sites.

Similarly, the supermarket is never un-local, in as much as supermarket chains deploy local branches within specific locales, at the same time as its goods and capital circulates globally. The supermarket is globally constructed, but locally deployed. At this point, I believe it is possible to view IET and the local supermarkets as positive and negative facets of the same image of global capitalism. There is a dialectical movement which begins to occur, again, through 'traces' such as bamboo canes, sourced internationally, but planted, 'totally locally'.

This is an infrastructural argument about the way in which IETs project is moving, but it is possible to chase these debates back on to the cultural, superstructural landscape, particularly in some of the public discourses IET create. Under IET organiser Pam Warhurst's monologues there lies distinction. I wondered if the gender bias in IETs project risked reproducing the woman as the producer of food within its utopian discourse, or if they were trying to shift to a matriarchy. Marx and Engels' 'idiocy of the rural'[88] is a return to unproductive methods of sustenance and ultimately a long decline in health, education and culture.

Whether modern methods could provide a return to agrarian living without such a slide remains to be seen. Julie Guthman thinks not, but Roberto Sonnino is more positive, asking for further research, on a case-by-case basis. These are big questions, too big, and I am only interrogating the cultural landscape these larger questions sit upon here. But it is key to point out that, so far, ecological concerns do not threaten to erode the old hegemonic relationship between education, cultural knowledge, capital and land ownership. Actually, the real urge behind all of this, I suspect, is simply the urge to co-opt resources. But 'co-op' assumptions of community, which attempt to ignore the politics of land ownership, have simultaneously drawn and attempted to erase, for the observer, an ideological line.

At the root of all of this lies distinction. These are the real roots, the real 'pure' ground on which these processes sit. IET demarcate themselves in relation to, and away from, permaculture groups and the sustainable towns movement, and under this kind of partisanship lies an attempt to gain resources and to put themselves at the centre of the deployment of those resources. In a similar way, I used to demarcate my own cultural background, to deploy it in particular, nostalgic ways, taking cultural elements from my own history, in order to enter into discourses in my workplace, which were also part of a struggle for recognition and resources.

Whether claiming that voluntary agricultural labour is 'fun' is any less disingenuous than recruiting people through fear or new age spirituality is a moot point, I think. In any case, it isn't a question I can answer. But what I think emerges very clearly here is a sort of new non-conformism of the present, which sees labour as noble, there's a kind of Calvinist missionary zeal underpinning the project which remains unexamined, and it tends to elide the continuation of capitalism as an exchange system. Again, historically, this area always favoured co-ops over trade unionism.

Nick Brown complains about the sustainable towns movement using 'fear', at the same time as his biggest labour source works precisely through the fear of the consequences which would be triggered if they did not. Yet not all of these workers are completely reluctant. Nick described one community service worker to me whose parents once had a local farm. Strictly, this person shouldn't be on the site, as he's considered 'too dangerous', but Nick tells me he's 'been good as gold'. If that farm had been viable, he explains, this young man wouldn't be on the scheme now. Nick tells me how he is planting potatoes and watching for them coming up. He goes through the 'we've lost the skills' argument at this point again, saying 'frankly young people aren't taught to work, and that work is a good thing':

You can't eat your computer, there may be a handful of kids who can make a living making computer games... some are talented and lucky, but some have been given huge aspirations and aren't going to be able to fulfil them... you are told that anyone can do anything they want...

He thinks for a while, before saying 'and they coooould...' stretching out the last word, before concluding quickly, 'but it's not very likely.' Nick muses that there are young people in schools 'who don't know that they want to make stuff', and another, big unexamined question sits under this. Is the desire to do anything at all framed by existing cultural practices, or do cultural practices and changes in them frame those desires? De-industrialisation seems to lurk under the conversation here, specifically. There are also a bigger set of questions about whether work is intrinsically good on the current landscape, in which working practices have become fragmented, idiotic, scarce, pointless, brutalizing and in many cases quite literally senseless.

A sign board appeared at the IET Walsden site, a few months prior to the interview with Nick, which actually displayed some of his rhetoric. This raised heckles among some local working class people, and the site became immediately conflated with Gordon Rigg's garden centre:

> There's a sign up there by that land for Incredible Edible with "not all young people are high flyers" on it, saying they should volunteer... high fliers! If they work at Riggs on them wages they're never gonna be high fliers! [Arnold]

There is a further interesting moment in this regard, when Nick talks about 'being set up for failure'. Under this seems to lurk the closure of his own business. This seems to frame the way he talks about young people. Nick Brown's default email signature reads 'Ph.D, Chair, Incredible Edible Growing Ltd'. He also mentions his PhD in the interview, partly I think for my benefit, but I also sensed a map of his own resentments and disappointments emerging here. He says he got a PhD because he was engaged in the education system, 'but that doesn't happen anymore'.

Mary Clear also described the lack of prospects for MA and

PhD-holding young people to me, and in this I think we can sense the resentments of an expanded middle class which has stopped expanding.

Nick then talked about 'the people who know about chicken raising and slaughtering', telling me that the techniques 'are not in the books, I've read all the books, but there aren't any good books.' He tells me that IET are 'recreating that knowledge base', because 'it's 90% gone.' There's a striking mourning for 'the old ways' here, and the binary casting of IETs interests with computer games technology stood out.

A final moment flashed up, when Nick spoke about the transparency of knowledge. He told me that the people who know about chicken rearing and slaughter 'wouldn't think to write books about it', and simply carry the knowledge and cultural practices around with them, unexamined. This is where the interview ended, on this point about unexamined cultural practices operating through the people who possess them, who carry them out, and this was highly appropriate, because I could see this happening all the way through the interview, to the interviewee.

A complex jumble of ideologies emerged in just one short encounter here, which, when hooked up to some of the public, media discourses, radiating out of the IET project, create a set of paradoxes and tensions. The idea of providing community resources, but not going so far as to give people autonomy because they are not trusted, contains a fundamental, irresolvable tension, particularly in light of the fuzzy, 'feel good' empowerment rhetoric around the 'propaganda gardens' in Todmorden.

Walsden was feted as the biggest allotment growing territory in the region during WWI. We can see the boundary and border lines of the plots in Roger Birch's *Todmorden Album*, Volume 1. Yet here, the idea that the public may have drawn boundaries in a similar, allotment-style provision, was being used to justify IETs own boundary drawing on this site, literally, geographically, but also ideologically, and the way those ideological boundaries operated were equally paradoxical, because at the same time IETs media discourses proclaim that they 'trust people' and 'truly believe' that 'people are decent' and that this 'is a revolution', and that IET 'are gentle revolutionaries, and that everything IET do 'is underpinned by kindness.'[89] Here, again, is distinction, as those who can do the doing get on and do it, and as they do so, they loosely draw boundaries of distinction, they wall off the other, before attempting to render those walls invisible. In this sense, the 'propaganda gardens' are well-named, because they are one key way in which the IET project insiders attempt to erase the ideological lines they create as they place themselves 'inside' in the first place.

Trying to solve 'food security issues' under a traditional capitalist business model contains a fundamental tension, because organic practices strip growing of the elements of earlier forms of agribusiness practices which were put in place precisely to solve food security issues. The 'traces' which hit me, during my interview with Nick Brown, arrived via my ears. The blasts of powertool were agonistic divides between the interviewer and his suddenly recalcitrant interviewee, but they were also the flimsy partition walls between this endeavour, the 'pure', organic growing group, IET, and supposedly 'regular' capitalist agri-businesses, using 'oil based' methods.

The politics of land ownership – both Nick's, which enabled him to do free work, 'interesting stuff' – and the politics of land ownership of Gordon Riggs, who leased the land to IET for free, were equally paradoxical. Nick's freedom to roam was under-pinned by his status as a landlord, and the land on which he roamed freely was provided by rich capitalists, who took their surplus from the labour of workers in a garden centre down the road, and another in Rochdale. These garden centres source their goods from overseas, including regular deliveries of flowers from

Holland, and wooden garden furniture from China and Eastern Europe. I worked in the warehouse briefly and unpacked the boxes, which contained empty Polish beer bottles and Chinese newspapers. Again, local working class resentment can be detected here:

The Riggs, they're not horticulturalists are they? Buy for 50p sell for £1. It all comes from bloody China. [Alan]

Nick Brown told me how the owner of Gordon Riggs will lend IET their digger whenever they like, and I begin to think through the journey the diesel takes, flowing into the tank of the digger, paid for by other flows of capital and labour, but 'localised', rhetorically, by this other assemblage. IETs rather one-dimensional politics of labour were also elided by similar rhetoric, but, I would argue, their labour supply is fundamentally linked to much wider land ownership, capitalism and the global supply-and-demand questions for the area. After all, I had followed one research participant, Jean, right up to his enrolment in the Community Service scheme, and he may well have ended up working for IET. It was only by chance that he ended up in the bleakly ironic position of pricing up DVDs and other items in a charity shop. Jean went into criminal practices in the first place largely, although not completely, because of a lack of decent, available, local work.

The class assumptions I found here included the idea that labour was intrinsically noble, that working for free was viable and/or enjoyable. All of these paradigms must be handled dialectically, as they all hold contradictions, in fact to make those contradictions visible, contradictions which are already writhing under the surface of the discourses here, is to make dialectical work. The dialectical process is triggered by 'traces', blasts of white noise from a powertool – which is suddenly being employed both practically and socially – or by bamboo garden canes, traces of Chinese newspaper and the odd Polish beer bottle, inside a packing crate, itself unpacked from a shipping container.

Socially, culturally, under the conversation with Nick Brown there were traces of missionary zeal and messianism, auguries, shadows of earlier Christian ways of life, 'shadows of god' and nostalgified ideas about earlier forms of rural life. All these elements are present in IET's wider public and media discourses. These thin, cultural collages, and these shadows, were cast by the monolith of distinction. But under all of this I think, lies redemption. These cultural collages were made out of an intrinsic need to tame lives which are inevitably chaotic, to root in the rootless. And that is exactly, as I pointed out in my methodological and theoretical chapter, what lies under my own project, and under the practices of some of those we met in the last chapter. In this, I also carry a trace of missionary zeal in my desire to undertake this project in the first place.

These are the dialectics of deracinated localism. But here are also the dialectics of the future, as Julie Guthman explains, that:

> ...many of these projects emphasise consumer choice, localism, entrepreneurialism, and self-improvement demonstrates the extent to which food politics have been at the cutting edge of neoliberal regulatory transformations.[90]

For Guthman, the link to Marxism, via commodity fetishism, is a crucial point to make here, as she describes the way food is inevitably encountered as already-fetishised. This inevitably doubles back again to the politics of labour:

> Labor is one of the most significant mystifications attending food production, organic or otherwise. Despite common perceptions to the contrary, organic agriculture depends on the same racialized cheap labor and unsavory contracting

practices as conventional agriculture. Too many people are burying their heads in the sand on this issue. If organic farmers are heroes, as Alice Waters has said more than once, so are the men and women who actually plant, care for, and harvest the crops we all eat for heroically low wages. Can agriculture be sustainable in any meaningful way without providing a living wage for its labor?

Guthman's concerns are all equally applicable to 'green' Todmorden, they are what lie under its rhetoric.

22

Exploring the roots

All the different strands of discourse, which I have tried to illuminate here, wrapped around the IET project, create a complex mesh of conflicting desires and ideologies. Underneath IETs project lies a mix of class, gender, and racial assumptions, which are woven into the project and its advocacy. Particular kinds of historicism and futurology are being created at the same time. There is a complex interplay here, of localism and anti-local debates, around supermarketization and its opponents, around neo-liberalism and sustainability, gentrification, and what Darren Smith calls 'greentrification'.

IET often triggers a strong sense of alignment or dis-alignment, in class terms, whenever the subject of local production arises. There is a strong sense of alignment coming from middle class Todmordians, and dis-alignment from working class citizens. I also detected some of what Skeggs[91] has called 'dis-identification', which she applied to working class subjectivities, from some middle class voices involved in green projects, alongside much more straightforwardly positive identi-fication from them. This middle class 'dis-identification' – I bracket it here because Skeggs' term is such a specific usage – may have been performative to an extent, on display for a working class researcher, or at least one with a fairly broad accent, but not completely.

In terms of middle class 'dis-identification', I might want to cite James, a middle class man in his mid-40s who also recently set up a local organic food business, who expressed some cynicism to me – quite restrained and polite cynicism – in order to distance himself from the more excessive claims coming from local food producers, IET particularly. I told James that Warhurst had talked about small-scale capitalism on the radio, but he dismissed this as something to criticise them for, adding that 'they just aren't doing what they say, you go to the vegetable beds and there's not much there.' As he saw it, they should be more honest about being a limited company, and stop trying to put up a 'revolutionary' image. James told me, 'Pam's got her business in The Bear.' As he saw it, the IET project seemed to be a front for the other activities by its key players.

James then used the term 'slow food' to describe his own interest, and rarely mentioned co-ops or voluntarism. His 'take' on localised production was as a small-scale capitalist returning to manufacturing. James wasn't 'dis-identifying' with his (middle) class completely, but he was certainly distancing himself from elements of a particular form of middle class food production and its rhetoric, and this seemed to be underlined when he described IET as 'evangelistic'. This, it seemed, had a very similar function to the statements made by Nick Brown when he bracketed himself off from the permaculture 'new agers' and the sustainable towns movement, they all had similar objectives and concerns, but nonetheless boundaries were being drawn between them.

I think that we can map what Skeggs described as a kind of disarticulation of class onto middle class examples such as James. In fact, I would go one further, and suggest that the middle classes were literally starting to occupy – a buzz word at that point with the Occupy London group still outside St. Paul's Cathedral – the old territories of the working classes after the crash of 2008. But what they really occupy is a symbolic version of allotments and 'earthiness', which, via my descriptions from my own family, of the struggles of that life, we can see that they have little to do with the excessively cosy view of that way of life: The allotments have been 'occupied' by IETs project, not handed out to a wider public on a shared landscape. IET live their project as though it is a way of life, but it is a 'way of being', an interest community, which takes its symbolism from the mythologised surfaces of previous ways of life.

I am of course completely hijacking 'dis-identification' polemically here in order to explain how a middle class version of the concept might operate. Skeggs first deployed the term 'dis-identification' to describe how working class female research participants could not/would not identify in class terms, and instead they created a discourse around respectability. Savage, Silva and Warde later suggested that it is 'not clear whether dis-identification is restricted to those holding working-class identities. Are the middle classes, who presumably feel less stigmatised, less likely to dis-identify from class?' [92]

The answer to this question, for me, is 'no', but great care must be taken to weigh the gravities of these two different classes, and to understand the very different processes via which they construct their subjectivities. The most basic type of middle class distancing from IETs project manifested roughly in the form of 'Pam Warhurst is annoying', which could be a mix of jealousy and over-exposure to IETs rhetoric. I didn't find this surprising, or particularly interesting. But elsewhere, people quite heavily involved in 'localism' could also be found who distanced themselves from the project in more empirical terms, and this is where I became interested: James was the first one to do this, expressing scepticism about the evangelistic nature of the IET project, while weighing what could be found to pick for free with Warhurst's activities as a business owner.

In this mesh of alignments and dis-alignments, middle class 'greens' such as James, Nick Brown, Pam Warhurst and Mary Clear, are making themselves moral subjects, but in slightly different ways. This can be mapped onto Skeggs' term 'dis-identification', although these middle class subjects work their dis-identifying in a different direction, taking up opportunities, at the same time as they defend themselves from stigma, although I suspect that in James's case he was attempting to entirely occupy a zone – a former working class zone, manufacturing – which has now come to be seen in a quite romanticised, nostalgic way. At this point, a rash of 'blitz spirit' popular culture was circulating nationally, which seemed to tie in with what was happening locally, and Mary Portas's show The Bottom Line, shot in nearby Rochdale, was a highly romantic re-collaging of the industrial past, which painted factory life as rosy, at the same time as it often stigmatised the working classes as 'indolent' and conveniently omitted large parts of political history in regard to de-industrialization. All of this should be opposed by the new community researcher, at the same time as the complex processes at play are mapped.

I have already described James, who once worked in IT, for the Halifax Bank of Scotland (HBOS), the now-disgraced bank, now labelling his cheeses with his HBOS business cards.[93]

More straightforwardly, James's new business, historically couched in the 'localism' of 2012, has been set up with money skimmed from a business bloating out of control in 2008. There is a very large historical juncture here, which plays out, not only in the very narrow valley I am researching, but also globally, and it is triggered by tiny details, 'traces'. This kind of narrative is the real framing story for the 'greentrification' here, it is what is really happening under its mythified surfaces.

The return of the middle classes to localised production, re-occupying sites – literally in some cases – evacuated of working class life, is a return precisely to re-create the sequence James has just witnessed. As they do so they take on and jettison certain aspects of social class, agonistically, to bracket themselves off from others in the field, or to align themselves with others with whom they can work. They try to root themselves in an inherently rootless world. These processes are not simple conversations, they are inherently contradictory, and those contradictions can never be simply separated off and examined. But what we need to do here is produce a risky and critical ethnography of those processes, which always tries to get under the surface rhetoric of groups such as IET.

CONCLUSIONS

23

Returning to epistemology

Here I want to summarise the need for 'several' returns to community research, before exploring the key elements of the book's title – in three sections – to examine my central concept of 'deracinated localism', a concept which is tied to the erosion and cohesion of 'conviction'. I will then explore the 'austere times' element of my work, by discussing 'degentrification', and then I shall make some final remarks, which summarise the bigger sweep of this research.

Here, I have explained that small towns can no longer be viewed as discrete entities. They probably never could, but in 2013 they certainly should not be. In this sense, I want this book to be a proposal towards a new body of literature on the sociology of community, as well as a proposal for a revived, qualitative ethnographic practice for small towns. This means that 'returning to' community research should mean continuing to travel to small towns to live in them and to study them, but not to view them as 'whole'.

The key point I am making is that the 'transnational' of migration, flows of capital and technology, is not something to be accessed only in urban centres, where it is somehow 'seen', but it can be accessed in small towns, by examining the ways people 'get by', it can be seen in the intermittency of flows of capital and access to labour, as well as the ways in which incomers attempt to localise themselves, embed themselves into the landscape, access resources and symbolically cloak themselves with 'the local'. It can be seen in the changing moral dimensions of community, in the increasing activities of different ethnic groups in civic life, and in its extreme racists: These are, literally, all dialectical figures.

These processes, as people try to root themselves in a globally lifted-out local, I have called 'deracinated localism'. I have also argued that these processes and their contradictions need to be assessed via a return to a particular kind of dialectical thinking. I have also made a claim for a return to 'the familiar', which need not be narcissistic, at the same time as it retains a politicised, ideological dimension. A return, in some ways then, to 'social criticism'.

I have argued that the rural and urban are such fudged containers, such compromised epistemologies, that they must be re-assessed, again, dialectically, but specifically in terms of how the rural and urban are raised in order to, for instance, resist a stigmatised other, or to 'naturalise' oneself in a landscape. At the same time, I tried to describe how the ultimate logic of this landscape is that of the public and private. This initial chapter on the public and private framed all my subsequent ethnographic sections, in that they were all then trying to dynamite the epistemologies of community which I found to be historicised or unhelpful, for instance, 'working and not working'. I also deliberately placed the section on 'getting by' forms of life in Todmorden next to the section on green localism, because the green activists there raise the symbols of 'getting by', at the same time as they face a class divide, over which lie the working classes and excluded of Todmorden, who 'get by' in an entirely different order.

I also tried to show how traces of earlier social life exists here, although in a ghostly form, for instance the puritanism of the green locals, mirroring old forms of Methodism. At the same time, naturalised spaces such as the park in Todmorden are often seen to be 'of the local', despite being products of late empire, and yet simultaneously, incomers from the history of empire are seen as 'alien'.

This book has been largely about locating such contradictions, through assessing problematic epistemologies, which can be found operating in all these different groups. For instance, via the bumper sticker, 'Totally Locally', with its flipside of 'not local', a purity and toxicity discourse emerged, which saturated all the other discourses in this book.

My subsequent ethnographic explorations all tackled this idea: I began this book talking about public solutions to private problems, and one big conclusion here is that 'local solutions' to global problems, in places which are deemed, culturally, to be more 'of the local' – as Todmorden is – are going to be limited in their effectiveness, at the same time as the contests over that effectiveness and the struggles for resources around them will partly structure the local in a very real way. Again, this is why dialectical thinking is needed.

The media circuits beyond Todmorden often project very particular images of the place, for instance the lesbian drift from Hebden Bridge, or the green activists, but these cultural changes are often elided in favour of the material the media fetishises and presents. The debates around supermarketization work in a similar way, as they also contained the attempt to return to a 'local' which will always be uprooted, and so a further purity and toxicity discourse could be accessed here, again, dialectically, as it was a dialogue of often quite extreme contradiction. Again, the 'alien' of supermarket capital was often being set against the 'Totally Local' of the market stalls in the centre of town, which were themselves produced by flows, rather than stability. The nationalism which could be encountered in popular culture such as 'Keep Calm and Carry On', I framed in the same way. There was an attempt to adhere to something solid, something 'central', which was actually a cultural collage which consisted of disparate elements. The local neo-Nazi provided the starkest example of this.

24

Several returns to community research

My attempt to collapse some unhelpful binaries, and therefore re-arrange the epistemological furniture of community research a little, which I have just explained, also has ramifications for the language of the subject, and I am arguing here for my more dialectical approach to be taken up: For instance, Graham Crow describes Rosser and Harris's 1965 'The Family and Social Change': '...in which the contrast between "the cohesive society" and "the mobile society"' is explored. Crow is right to claim that it prefigures individualisation debates and globalisation research, but this only arrives in retrospect, and the binary set-up is finally the paradigm that I still take issue with: The cohesive and mobile are dialectically meshed; Adrian Ashton makes himself 'cohesive' within a Christian family unit, which he repro-duces daily, and he keeps this stable through his constant mobilization of self, both physical – travelling all over the country and outside it – and symbolically, in terms of networking people and institutions. He is both mobile and 'cohesive', as is Todmorden as a town.[95]

I began my work here with Graham Crow's retrospective of fifty years of community research[96] which itself is now over ten years old: The 'fifty years of theorization' of his title are now sixty. Crow asked us to work '...in a way that attempts to discover the interconnected nature of the various social forces at work' in any given place. Community studies 'are holistic', he says, 'and by this token are able to engage with several big ideas at once'. We can revisit Ronald Frankenberg, looking down on his border village houses in 1957, wondering what was going on there, wishing to know.[97]

The private is finally where all the other big binaries I have explored here are settled, the slow and fast, the rural-urban. It's possible to gaze on beautiful views out of windows here, which tell you nothing about the crippling anxieties experienced by those who live with those views each day. 'The holistic', for me, is far from the point.

We should also be wary of the 'holistic' as declared on the ground. At this point, particular conversations stick in the mind, and the man who told me 'my neighbour absolutely hates me, he thinks I'm the laziest man alive, because I'm a fireman', is one. Yet locally, there's a kind of exhibitionism of 'the holistic'. But when people start declaring 'holism' obsessively, like 'community', it is probably in trouble. This last point is probably speculative, but what is not speculative is the clear evidence that people are displaying themselves as completed subjects here, and the rhetoric of localism connected to spirituality is often tied to this. It is possible to glimpse something like a cultural unconscious through these kinds of declarations, which sometimes say roughly the opposite of what they state.

This is often revealed by questions that cause irritation, for instance my question to the green activist about feudalism. The same thing could be seen in the denial of a recession, or explanations of personal circumstances as not tied to wider forces. It was possible to then catch people extrapolating these assumptions – which are all essentially defensive psychological moves – way beyond the local and personal, into some of the messy, contradictory explanations of the wider world I have laid out here in my empirical chapters.

Community research must tackle these complexes now, community studies itself must be preserved and transformed, dialectically, because the social relations in the places it goes to have also been preserved and transformed. 'Several' returns, means going back to the subject to cut out earlier aspects of its approaches, as the new situation dictates. But 'return' also means revisiting some historical approaches in order to rescue them, dialectics in particular. History actually, asks for community studies to be refigured, not me. It has fallen behind its subject, 'community' has been producing uprooted forms of localism, rather than 'cohesive' ones, for some time, but community research still sometimes tries to study cohesion as a straight-forward, rather than dialectical paradigm. But we also need, finally, to reconnect community as it is experienced, with the critical accounts of community we can produce as qualitative ethnographic researchers, by looking for traces of alterity, and via dialectical thinking.

Imran and his family also make themselves 'cohesive' through global shuttling and interactive communications, and he is equally 'of' Todmorden and its landscape, in a fairly patriotic and declaredly 'rural' way, talking of mountain biking around the moors in between his local gym instructor work. There is a dialec-tical, rather than simplistic relationship between rootedness and its opposite: Cohesion and mobility are linked, they do not have the oil and water quality they are often viewed to possess. The flipside to Adrian and Imran are the thoroughly, grindingly alienated, who worked in, for instance, nearby Halifax and Rochdale, who rarely left Todmorden, except to go to work, and yet felt that they had no part to play in the town, as counterpoints to these utterly elated, loyal, patriotic Todmordians, who were sometimes only rarely there. You could not identify any of these things, through, for instance, distance travelled to work statistics, which are easily accessible through the ONS website. Mike Savage's work on the mobile and cohesive goes little further than Rosser and Harris's, it adds 'elective' and other paradigms, but it appears to view these aspects as almost Lego-brick components in the social landscape, rather than fundamentally meshed struc-tures. IET are an elective group attempting to 'go-cohesive', something which is nonetheless experienced as cohesion from within. This is a dialectical assemblage, to declare it as one or the other is not the point, but for me it is the point to describe the strange, inside-outside view one gets through engagement with these groups, before pulling back.

In a way then, this has been a narrative of extremes, as I have focused in on particular examples, which spoke to my theme of 'deracinated localism'. I didn't just find black marketeers and neo-Nazis, I also found what one might describe as 'average' Todmordians. However, a racist, who believes in a theoretical 'Britain for the British', despite working in global engineering, indeed visiting disparate parts of the globe for that work, and screams at Asian taxi drivers who are navigating at a regional level, when his nationally mobile son has been caught doing over 100 mph on the motorway, and who then, finally, turns out to have close Asian friends, cannot be described as 'an anomaly' in my view, but actually something closer to the 'characterisation' of the current small town post-community local, which Crow is both keen for us to look for and nervous about the problems inherent in declaring. Close Asian friends are not a barrier to the new genetically modified racism, which has morphed into a more virulent strain, like some psychological super-flu. Until thrown out of his own party, the neo-Nazi didn't seem to think that Asian fascists were a barrier to his own Hitlerism.

In the same way, it seems that the lack of money a person has is no barrier to declarations of the new class, in fact if anything, middle class-ness here is raised symbolically via the signifiers of a rustic, fingerless-gloved poverty and 'humility', which conceals as much as it reveals. All of these previously simple, large slabs, designating social groups have become 'complexes'. But from the inside, for these people, their views are 'cohesive', rather than 'complex' or 'contradictory'.

Crow is nervous, I guess, to declare any kind of 'characterisation', precisely because of the risks we face in returning to the large, slab-like declarations – the 'isms' – which he outlines as being misleading. He does not want to re-inscribe any one figure as a mask for complexity. But I am prepared to risk controversy over the issue here, and in any case dialectical thinking deals with it: This 'complex' is the figure I found here – and the psychological connotations of that word are appropriate – not some neatly categorisable 'elective' or 'indigenous', but someone who is both. People who are clearly 'indigenous' in that they are rooted in this place, but 'elective' at the same time, in that they select the slices or fragments of ideology they collage together on a daily basis, some consciously, others much less so. Simple terms such as 'elective' cannot describe someone really messy, who is often as likeable on a personal, everyday level as he or she is contestable on an ideological one: 'Complex' is both the mask and what is under it.

In some ways, this has been a pedagogy of extremes, but these extreme examples still stand as a model for perhaps less markedly contradictory figures, because roughly, the processes which were active in the racist figures were active by degrees all over the social landscape in Todmorden: It is to these contradictory processes we must hold. This is a further big conclusion here. These contradictions frame my concept of 'deracinated localism'. Deracinated localism is the attempt to resist neoliberalism, at the same time as neoliberalism is inevitably reproduced at a local level. The terms of reference between the two processes are being blurred so much in some places that the attempts to resist either end up being assimilated by those processes, or they become very contradictory.

Again, I have provided some perhaps extreme examples of contradiction here, but IET are a mix of public grants and private sales, underpinned by voluntary labour, and in this they could be described as essentially neoliberal. The local Labour Party are caught in the same double-bind, they are local, but trapped within the iron cage of Labour central's neoliberalism. I could have written a chapter on my immersion in local Labour politics, but simply explaining the rigidity they are trapped in will suffice. The supermarket chaos is economic, it is produced by economic hedging, store sizes and catchment areas, and this is geographical, and this does plays out in the local geography – or rather, like my argument for conceptualizing the place around a lack of flows – it leaves spaces abject, derelict and empty, although some anti-supermarket campaigners argue this is better than having a supermarket. Zygmunt Bauman describes the divorce between 'power' that is global and 'politics', which is local and nothing, it seems, can overcome this split.[98] This is the biggest dialectical figure here, the sad *'aufheben'*, and it is a sadness that all the figures I encountered on this landscape are trying to defend themselves from.

25

Deracinated localism – the erosion and cohesion of 'conviction'

At its heart, 'deracinated localism' explores the simultaneous erosion and cohesion of 'conviction'. In this long, spectacular hangover from the industrial era, we are seeing the lingering ghost of the subject with convictions: 'Conviction' also means 'to make prisoner', and in some ways this is appropriate, as people were 'trapped in place' here previously, and some still are, mentally. So to think of these figures as 'now released' would be too simplistic. But being in-between conviction and release is what generates much of the contradiction here.

Crow also states that community research has historically been about identifying trends, and that this has some merit, though it is problematic. If there is a trend to be witnessed here, it is perhaps that there is no longer a real clear sense of 'the established' and 'the outsider'. This, on the one hand means that a kind of social loosening has occurred since the industrial era – there is nothing new in this statement – and on the other hand it means that very fierce forms of symbolic loyalty, 'conviction', which once might have at least resembled symbolic violence, are dissipated. But this hasn't necessarily been replaced with anything more liberating or less agonistic either.

There was a profound sense of working class ambivalence to 'othered' cultural forms here, much less so than straight out antagonism, which was nonetheless equally effective as a form of resistance, and could be traced on the other side of its formal non-dialogue (ignoring entire groups isn't really a conversation). This seemed to be the case when listening to groups with their own agency and agenda complain that the working classes 'don't get it', or dislike them, although when asked for the details of this, the answer was often that the antagonism was communicated subliminally. This seemed to speak most strongly to the 'loosening' which has occurred since the decline of industry. So, I think that while the paradigms of 'established' and 'outsider' may have been to an extent overcome, they are also, to an extent, preserved as well. They have been negated, transformed. So again, I want to replace Crow's idea about identifying trends with finding the dialectical processes active within any one given figure. This big conclusion should be more than clear at this point.

Some people are sticking by their old convictions, but their opinions, their subjectivities even – like a piece of twenty ton factory machinery – are too heavy, and they risk crashing through the floor, because the social floor of the old world has decayed, it is weak. The opposite of this is a kind of relativism beyond itself. It's almost as though these two poles have not settled into some middle register yet, and this seems to cut across class.

I spoke to a very posh Republic member – the campaign for the abolition of the monarchy – who saw her attendance at the Buckingham Palace Jubilee Celebration as unproblematic. She is a product of 'electivity', all choices have become opened-out, levelled, all are fair game, this is the laissez-faire of the social. But there was a kind of unconsciously incubated, retrospective attempt to sketch 'conviction' back in. At the same time – genuinely – she is a committed 'localist'. So there isn't a clear-cut, elective-indigenous binary, people here are trying make their elective choices authentic. This is not something which only happens in Todmorden, of course, but the form it takes in places like this, 'rustification', for instance, aesthetic returns to 'old ways', are very specific.

So this idea of the contradictory or not-contradictory, which I am generating here, finally also needs to be dialectically overcome. This is another big point of my conclusion. Life experienced via these excessively heavy or excessively light, relative subjectivities, are all experienced as coherent. We need to finally get to a place where we can see that it all 'works', but that this 'working' contains jarring contradictions. But I stop short at, for instance, Bourdieu's assertions that we can reach a higher objectivity.[99] This goes for me, the 'researcher', as much as for the subjects of the research. The irrational nature of our own culture can only be seen from outside, and I did get half-way outside, and it is cold there, but still, there is no final binary of the rational or irrational here, the adjusted or not adjusted, nor then, is there some final place called 'objectivity' either, and this, for me, goes for Hegel as much as for Bourdieu, although the latter talks of meshed problems, which the researcher is dragged along by, and this makes a lot of sense. It may be useful to revisit Walter Benjamin at this point:

> The true picture of the past flits by. The past can be seized only as an image which flashes up at the instant when it can be recognized and is never seen again. ... To articulate the past historically does not mean to recognize it "the way it really was". It means to seize hold of a memory as it flashes up in a moment of danger. [100]

However, this does not mean that we should stop making strident, politicised accounts of places such as Todmorden, far from it. What we need are potent cultural batteries to try to illuminate the forces of history and their effects upon our own lives, but we also need to refuse solipsistic accounts of community, as well as the theologies of both global capitalist and local certainty, in order to try to move towards a stronger history, which perhaps counter-intuitively takes its strength from acknowledging the impossibility of the production of certainty. At the same time, we need to produce forms of 'truthness', forceful proposals which illuminate how all lives under global capitalism – rich, middle and poor – are shaped by forces which are neither rational or fair: This is also what I have tried to do here.

It was perhaps easier to live in 'conviction' when confined to one group within solid walls, as in the industrial period, with its seemingly heavy certainties, which proved to be as lightweight, ultimately, as any other part of history. The problem is how to maintain conviction on an uncontained landscape, the processes of its making and remaking are so diffuse that we now live within clear walls: 'clear' as in transparent, illusory; but also giving the illusion of simplicity and 'naturalness'. This is also Bauman's project, of course, but I have tried to produce a detailed account of how that plays out in a very specific place, which also puts the dialectical approach back into the work.

The older, perhaps 'easier' paradigms of social class – like sides in the Cold War – have been eroded, and yet social life retains some of the lingering structure of 'conviction', of its time in that contained past, long after that past has gone. 'Containerization' can be thought of as a metaphor, but only if one inverts it, because when the metal boxes began containing objects, they did so to distribute them more widely and quickly across the globe. To use the language of Deleuze-Guattari[101] capitalism deterritorializes in order to territorialize, but it does not do so to trap people or objects in one place on any landscape, all of which are becoming steam. There is a boiling, a painful transition as we enter another phase of global movement, and here are some of the irrational symptoms, which are impossible attempts to stop the boiling: This is what it is to attempt resistance here. One reaction is to 'become relative' at the same time as retaining conviction, to cling on to the failing marriages of past allegiance – and sometimes this can be seen in the traces of real failing marriages – as those convictions become harder and harder to maintain.

But this applies to me just as much as the subjects of the

research. When I arrived in Todmorden, I joined and then left the Labour Party, as I couldn't maintain 'conviction' in there. It was impossible to ever square the circle of local Labour and the statements of Labour Party central figures such as Liam Byrne. 'Conviction' in the local was constantly eroded by the contradictions of the wider assemblage it was hooked to. One response to this is to slam down some excessively heavy, immovable certainties, which now crash through the weakened social floor. Some local political figures still do this.

The attempt to create holism is all over the landscape, but these attempts often only reveal the nature of the landscape of desire here, and, as in analysis, by inverting them: The testimonies to holism actually often tell us about its lack, not its arrival. The search for coherence, for 'lineage', continues here. Football talk seemed to be placed against the 'on and off' I described earlier, as it gave a constant set of cyclical 'seasons', against which the fragmentation might fade a little. You couldn't get this by interviewing people, or statistics, but you got it by hanging around a lot.

But all of this is experienced as a coherent whole – it 'works', essentially, for the subjects of my research – they do not inhabit this view of deracinated localism, I can only see the jarring juxtapositions from outside, just as I can only see my own inherent contradictions through the eyes of another. But the existence of this 'coherent wholeness' does not invalidate my argument about the way in which the construct hangs together, and where it frays. These insights, I want to argue, don't say anything pejorative about its continued 'cohering' for the subjects, with all their struggles acknowledged. An 'uncontained whole' of opposites emerges by looking at the material of this research from inside-out, and then outside-in, and this is perhaps the final dialectic. But this 'uncontained whole' is not 'holism', this is something quite different, which the Hegelian *aufheben* is appropriate to capture, it is a contradictory assemblage.

In some ways, my work has been extreme, in its location of contradiction. But in another sense, my work is not a pedagogy of extremes at all, because it actually tries to overcome the simplistic binary 'on/off' questions of, for instance, whether people are working or not working, insiders or outsiders, urban or rural. The temptation which needs to be resisted here is that of asking if this 'new situation', in class terms, for instance, is a glass half full or empty. I prefer to think in terms of a prism, which we need to turn over, from the perspectives of various viewers. Change is dialectical, especially community change. Change here is always negation and preservation, loosenings and migrations, making and re-making the face of one larger surface.

However, this advice, that we view things as 'complexes', should not fragment the political dimensions of what we find here either, and the struggles of the working classes, under-classes, and sole female parents – and female workers generally – are all getting gradually harder. The current changes to working tax credits and a whole host of other central government 'austerity' diktats are creating this situation. But the often nauseating cultural messages raised to counter the situation locally are undetectable to statistical analysis, and, I would argue, they are as powerful a dimension of the 'wellbeing' or otherwise of small towns as are the tiny trickles of capital they are linked to. My final comment here is that as we advance into viewing the 'complexes' of community we should not leave political commitment behind.

With this last point in mind, the final part of the title of this book is 'austere times', and it was inevitable that the crash of 2008, just before I began this work, would frame my research in some way. Crow also claims that community studies have '…a solid track record as testing grounds for general theories of social change, in which there is the potential to confound expectations and force the re-thinking of those theories.' I hope I have at least begun to address his advocacy here, by beginning to think through the cultural landscape after the crash, as we move into 'austerity'. Crow also states that:

> ...community studies have the capacity to show that social change does not unfold in the deterministic fashion in which abstract theories like those of industrialization, medicalization and globalization are open to being read.[102]

I strongly side with this. New, large sociological paradigms are starting to emerge after the crash of 2008, 'degentrification' being the most interesting one for my purposes.[103] 'Degentrification' may be the latest version of a term like 'de-traditionalization', which Crow also mentions favourably in review, but those terms always obscure at least as much as they reveal. In local figures who once worked in banking and similar industries, who are symbolically detoxifying themselves by moving into organic food production and other business start-ups, with the 'ethical' declared at least on an aesthetic level, we can see something like 'degentrification', but the term conceals the fact that this is the continuation of gentrification, which is essentially being under-written, excused even, via these symbolic recalibrations. The new middle classes are making themselves moral and moralizing subjects in particular kinds of ways, at the same time as they place themselves in positions of relative authority and power on the landscape, over and above a stigmatised neo-proletarian other. The fingerless-gloved symbolism is a cover. Care needs to be taken not to render terms such as 'degentrification' as simplistic, common sense paradigms, when degentrification and austerity can be used on the ground as alibis.

So, I will add to my advocacy that we dynamite old epistemologies, the addition of exploration of new ones such as 'degentrification', but as complexes. Amanda Ravetz's work in Todmorden[104] was about The State, declining agriculture, and old farming traditions. What I'm not saying here is that those 'older' things are undetectable now, they are: As I wrote this section, Roger Birch was about to publish a personal monograph, which traced the Barker family and their agricultural practices – which are just about still clinging on – from the eighteenth century to the present. What I am saying here is that the qualities of the social world – for most people – are not adequately reflected, in 2013, by this kind of description, even though it is possible to come to this town and do that describing. These symbolic inscriptions on the landscape present unconsciously whitened historical narratives, which many of the contemporary 'localist' endeavours are placed in, they place, for instance, old patriarchal concern in newly gendered paradigms, which incubate older forms of Methodism, which have migrated over via the co-operative movement, via the language of 'the saved' and wider apocalyptic references.

This is what I mean by 'complex', but what describes the conditions of life here for most people is 'deracinated localism', the unseen divorce of local and global power and politics, which can often only manifest itself as a symptom, because of its funda-mental invisibility.

On one level, all these new strains of communitarian advocacy around 'localism' morally other themselves from that which they are ultimately part of.

Yet on the other hand, they do not see the other at all, a figure such as Jean is as off their social radar as they are off his. Incredible Edible Todmorden and Jean were both undertaking forms of relatively anarchic informal labour, but one is praised and the other is shamed, in fact almost gaoled. I also found retired ladies knocking out good copies of Cath Kidston products, without the logo, for church craft fairs. There are complex and contradictory assemblages of informal labour and 'getting by' here, which more often than not do not recognise each other and sit, not on some evenly-applied legal system, but in the enclosures of older cultural assumptions which need to be revisited, but, it seems, in places like these, rarely are. This is also what I have tried to do here.

I need to make it very clear that all of this is not to put down the genuinely positive practical work put in by local and localist groups at all, but it is to describe the 'complex' social processes which those practices are tied to – culturally – and here is another contradiction which cannot be simply 'solved', these assemblages are half provision and half foreclosure, in a dialectical bind which cannot ever be neatly settled. The key point I am making here is that they can be better described by ethnographers of small town life in future, and this is a key part of my conclusion.

26

Final remarks

What I have done here, at the very broadest level, is to explain how Todmorden is a landscape entirely framed by flows of capital, weak or strong. It is a node in a global field, rather than a globalising force, yet at the same time, local community groups and figures attempt to sidestep this by 'rooting' themselves into place in various, largely symbolic ways. I have tried to represent these attempts to root against the uprooting global forces, those defensive moves instinctively placed against an unseen global power. A key point I am making is that this defensive symbol-making can only remain rhetorical, rather than effective as a deterrent. All these attempts to be a central force in a central place are saturated in contradiction, and to show this has been one main drive of this book.

But this is also just one part of the dialectic. On one hand, it would be possible to say that the 'Keep Calm and Carry On' Jubilee parade and the wooden shrines to beehives are all symptoms: They are the twitches of a zombie subject. They are sad songs sung at the so-called 'end of history'. When I began this work, I was strongly resisting 'community' as a zombie category, a term Ulrich Beck applies to the family, but now I cannot deny its veracity. I hovered around one of the Incredible Edible Propaganda Gardens, as a couple in their late-60s picked some onions out. 'Whistling in the dark, this lot', he said, 'but I'll have the veg'. He chuckled and walked away, an icon of Lancastrian working class self-interest, something that is far from inactive in younger generations.

All these groups were attempting to bracket themselves apart, to make themselves 'authentic' subjects at the same time as the global, essentially transnational landscape unfolded their attempts, often invisibly. They were all attempting to make defensive moves against what are essentially uprooting forces, by trying to root themselves symbolically. They were trying to identify or construct a 'locale' for themselves. This is why 'deracinated localism' is essential as a concept for community research now.

I have tried to show how those attempts to root in place, 'authentically', are largely rhetorical, at the same time as they are experienced from within 'as authentic'. I have tried to provide counterpoints to these essentially 'ways of being' forms of community, by locating and describing the 'ways of life' experienced by those who struggle to live in an area where flows of capital are weak or stuttering, away from a metropolitan centre, as what gentrification exists in the area largely passes them by. These figures do not live on the same landscape in some cosy or 'holistic' way, in fact, the one dis-accumulates as the other accumulates, and this, ultimately, is their real symbiotic relationship, and the political dimension of this book. Here we see history opening again after the amnesia of the bubble years, but again, the idea that people are now 'waking up' needs to be resisted, until it can be proven that they are not simply falling into older dreams.

But this is only one side of the picture, it is real enough, but it has to be reconnected with the way in which the psychological investments in the beehives and bunting work for those involved. I think there is, after Gilroy, with his notion of 'imperial hauntings', a very real mourning for a rapidly eroding post-World War Two consensus, but there is also a very real psychological 'getting by' in it all, which is no less important than the economic 'getting by' being done by Jean, selling shifty DVDs, or those who frequent the flea market. We have to finally connect these two things up – the positive and negative, cultural and economic – via a simultaneous distancing and immersion, which allows one to see the 1940s lipstick, the traces which force the kind of unconscious yearnings in local and localist cultures to be revealed, at the same time as we acknowledge that it all, somehow, 'works'.

This, again, is 'holism' here, it is not the holism of a completed subject, but a slowly transforming, historically-produced subject, which is the product of several sets of sometimes conflicting drives. These positive aspects must be seen as inseparable from the other side, what we might be tempted to describe as 'naïve', or perhaps 'politically-unproductive', following a heavily Marxist line: We should always resist this temptation, at the same time as we re-commit ourselves to politicised research. These 'localisms' may now sit on top of the landscape – they are not embedded in it – but they are experienced as rooted.

ENDNOTES

1. See Heywood, Heywood and Jennings (1996) *A History of Todmorden*. Otley: Smith Settle. See also Brian Law (1995) *The Fieldens of Todmorden – A Nineteenth Century Business Dynasty*. Littleborough: Kelsall.

2. John Greenwood (2007) 'Castle mystery as monks quit' Todmorden News, August 30.

3. E.P. Thompson (1963) *The Making of the English Working Class*. Harmondsworth: Pelican.

4. See C. Wright Mills (1970 [1959]) *The Sociological Imagination*. Harmondsworth: Pelican, as well as Zygmunt Bauman (2002) 'Individually, Together' in Beck and Beck-Gernsheim's (2002) *Individualization*. London: Sage. This idea of 'borders' maps on to my own personal practice, as I undertook much of this research half in and half out of funding, half in and out of academia, half in and out of the disciplines of documentary photography and sociology: Submitting this manuscript to Zero Books became almost inevitable later, with its own borderline position; intellectual, but not academia.

5. Savage, et al (2012) *The Great British Class Survey*, presentation at York University.

6. See Stephen Houlgate (ed., 1998) *The Hegel Reader*. Oxford: Blackwell and Kojève, A. (1969) *Introduction to the Reading of Hegel*. Ithaca: Cornell University Press. My understanding of Hegel hinges on long, fruitful conversations with my friend Mark Rainey in Manchester. Without our discussions, I would not have taken Hegel on in this way. I am indebted to him. Mark currently blogs here: http://edifyingdiscourse.wordpress.com/

7. Marx (1976 [1867]) *Capital Volume 1*. Harmondsworth: Penguin. Page 287.

8. Again, see Kojève (1969) *Introduction to the Reading of Hegel*. Ithaca: Cornell University Press.

9. Adorno (1951 [2005]) *Minima Moralia*. London: Verso.

10. Adorno (1951 [2005]) *Minima Moralia*. London: Verso. Page 50.

11. For Kant, space and time are infinite and therefore unknowable.

12. Adorno (1990 [1966]) *Negative Dialectics*. New York: E.B. Ashton.

13. Fredric Jameson (in eds., Hardt and Weeks, 2000) *The Jameson Reader*. London: Blackwell. Williams' ad hoc base-and-superstructure essay is in (ed., Higgins, 2001) *The Raymond Williams Reader*. Oxford: Blackwell.

14. Barthes (1984 [1980]) *Camera Lucida*, London: Flamingo, and Walter Benjamin (1999 [1940]) 'Theses on the Philosophy of History' and 'The Task of the Translator', in *Illuminations*, London: Pimlico. See also Jameson (in eds., Hardt and Weeks, 2000) *The Jameson Reader*. London: Blackwell. Derrida's (1967 [1980]) *Writing and Difference*, London: Routledge, also contains work on 'the trace'.

15. Walter Benjamin (1999 [1940]) 'Theses on the Philosophy of History' and 'The Task of the Translator', in *Illuminations*, London: Pimlico. See also my paper on HBOS (2009) 'Occupation Health' in *Social Alternatives*, Vol.28, No.1. Australia: University of the Sunshine Coast.

16. Again, see Heywood, Heywood and Jennings (1996) *A History of Todmorden*, Otley: Smith Settle, and Brian Law (1995) *The Fieldens of Todmorden*, Littleborough: Kelsall.

17. Peter Dicken (2002) 'Global Manchester: from globaliser to globalised' in (eds. Peck and Ward) *City of Revolution*, University of Manchester Press. I have also written about the way in which nuclear innovations incubated in the town have rebounded symbolically on its landscape, in the form of a CND graffito, traces of which can still be seen on the

Stoodley Pike Monument. For that argument, please see Urbis Research Forum Review, Issue 1, which can be downloaded here: http://urbisresearchforum.files.wordpress.com/2010/04/vol1_issue3_landscapes1.pdf

18. Todmorden News, 25/08/2011

19. Amanda Ravetz (2001) *Vision, Knowledge and the Invention of Place in an English Town*. Unpublished PhD thesis, University of Manchester, John Rylands library.

20. David Harvey (1990) *The Condition of Postmodernity*. Oxford: Blackwell.

21. Williams in (ed., Higgins, 2001) *The Raymond Williams Reader*. Oxford: Blackwell.

22. Sarat Maharaj (2010) '"Small change of the universal": beyond modernity?' *British Journal of Sociology*, Vol.61, No.3. Oxford: Blackwell.

23. For overviews of the community research field I will direct you to Gerard Delanty's (2010) *Community*, second edition, London: Routledge. Informed readers may notice similarities between my descriptions of tracing object-interrelations and Callon and Latour's work, but Latour refuses a dialectical approach, and so I side much more strongly with Daniel Miller's writing in this area, for instance, see his (2010) book *Stuff*, Cambridge: Polity. I do take Latour's criticisms of what he calls 'sociologists of the social' seriously though, for which see (2005) *Re-assembling the Social*, Oxford: OUP, and add to these Ulrich Beck's warnings about the risks of 'methodological nationalism', for instance (2002) 'The Cosmopolitan Society and its Enemies', *Theory, Culture & Society*, London: Sage. Vol.19, No.1.

24. Adorno (1990 [1966]) *Negative Dialectics*. New York: E.B. Ashton.

25. Williams, Raymond (1989) 'Between Country and City' in *Resources of Hope*. London: Verso.

ENDNOTES

26. Smales, Lindsay (2011) 'Key Issues Relating to Sainsbury's Application for a Foodstore at Halifax Road, Todmorden'.

27. Birch, R. (1972, 1983, 1987, 1993, 2006 and 2011) *A Way of Life and Todmorden Album* Volumes 1-5. Todmorden: Woodlands. This volume is partly dedicated to Roger, who taught and inspired me.

28. Smith, Neil (2008) *Uneven Development: Nature, Capital and Production of Space*. Third Edition. University of Georgia Press.

29. Ravetz, Amanda (2001) *Vision, Knowledge and the Invention of Place in an English Town*. Unpublished PhD thesis, University of Manchester, John Rylands library. See also Edwards, Jeanette (1998) 'The Need for a "Bit of History": Place and Past in English Identity' in Lovell, N. (ed.) *Locality and Belonging*. London: Routledge.

30. Corrigan, Paul (Eds., Hall and Jefferson, 1976) 'Doing Nothing' in *Resistance Through Rituals*. London: Hutchinson.

31. Smith, Darren (1999) *The Revitalisation of the Hebden Bridge District: Gentrified Pennine Rurality*. Unpublished PhD thesis. Leeds: The University of Leeds.

32. Heywood, Heywood and Jennings (1996) *A History of Todmorden*. Otley: Smith Settle.

33. Salmi, Hannu (2008) *Nineteenth Century Europe – A Cultural History*. Cambridge: Polity.

34. Thompson, E.P. (1967) 'Time, Work-Discipline and Industrial Capitalism', in *Past and Present*, Vol.38, No.1. Oxford: OUP.

35. Aiken, John (1795) *Description of the Country from Thirty and Forty Miles around Manchester*. New York: Gale Ecco, Print On Demand.

36. Hanson and Rainey (2013) 'The Urbis Building as Looking Glass', in *Cultural Studies*, forthcoming. London: Routledge; goo.gl/of4iv

37. Hanson, Steve (2010c) 'Reading the Calder Valley and

Todmorden: Rural, Industrial, Nuclear' in the Urbis Research Forum Review, Vol.1, No.3. ISSN: 2042-034X. Download from: http://urbisresearchforum.files.wordpress.com/2010/04/vol1_issue3_landscapes1.pdf [accessed 20/11/11].

38. Lewis, Jez (2011) 'Keynote speech', Documenting Fictions conference, National Media Museum, Bradford [06/04/11].

39. Barker, Paul (2012) *Hebden Bridge: A Sense of Belonging*. London: Frances Lincoln, and on Thinking Allowed, BBC Radio 4 [09/05/12].

40. Frankenberg, Ronald (1967) *Communities in Britain*. Harmondsworth: Pelican. See also Woods, Michael (2005) *Rural Geography*. London: Sage.

41. Smith, Darren (1999) 'The Green Potential of West Yorkshire' in *Regional Review* Vol.8, No.2, published by the School of Geography, Leeds University, http://www.geog.leeds.ac.uk/ [accessed 20/02/2012].
Smith, Darren (2001) 'Socio-cultural representations of greentrified Pennine rurality' in the *Journal of Rural Studies*, Vol.17, No.4. See also note 31.

42. Savage, Mike (2010) *Identities and Social Change in Britain Since 1940 – the Politics of Method*. Oxford: OUP.

43. Low, Setha (2003) *Behind the Gates: Life, Security, and the Pursuit of Happiness in Fortress America*. London: Routledge.

44. Hanson and Rainey (2013) 'The Urbis Building as Looking Glass', in *Cultural Studies*, forthcoming. London: Routledge; goo.gl/of4iv

45. Frankenberg, Ronald (1967) *Communities in Britain*. Harmondsworth: Pelican.

46. ONS (2011) Office For National Statistics, Key figures for 2001 Census: Census Area Statistics.

47. Candeias, Mario (2008) 'Double precarisation of labour and reproduction – Perspectives of expanded (re)appropriation' from The Rosa Luxemburg Foundation:

www.rosalux.de/cms/fileadmin/wgdw_uploads/Double_precarisation.pdf [accessed 01/01/10].

48. Fenton & Dermott (2006) 'Fragmented Careers?' *Work, Employment and Society*. Vol.20, No.3, June 2006. London: Sage.

49. ONS (2011) Office For National Statistics, Key figures for 2001 Census: Census Area Statistics.

50. Pahl, Ray (1984) *Divisions of Labour*. Oxford: Blackwell. Page 119.

51. Restivo, Sal (2011) *Red, Black and Objective, Science, Sociology and Anarchism*. Farnham: Ashgate.

52. 'Peter' (2010) informal interview with the author. See also note 55, below.

53. Williams, Raymond (2001) *The Raymond Williams Reader* and Jameson, Fredric (2000) *The Jameson Reader*. Both London: Blackwell.

54. Althusser in Easthope & McGowan (eds., 2008) *A Critical and Cultural Theory Reader*. Maidenhead: Open University Press.

55. Whenever a single name has been given in square brackets, for instance, 'Alan', it has been changed.

56. Sennett, Richard (1998) *The Corrosion of Character*. London: W.W. Norton, and (2006) *The Culture of the New Capitalism*. New Haven: Yale.

57. Ravetz, Amanda (2001) *Vision, Knowledge and the Invention of Place in an English Town*. Unpublished PhD thesis, University of Manchester, John Rylands library.

58. Stenning (2005) 'Where is the Post-socialist Working Class?: Working-Class Lives in the Spaces of (Post) Socialism', in *Sociology*, 39; 983. London: Sage. See also Mittin (2005) a review in *Work, Employment and Society*. Vol.19, No.1: 193-4, March 2005. London: Sage, and Hyman, Scholarios & Baldry (2005) 'Getting on or Getting by?' *Work, Employment and Society*. Vol.19, No.4, December 2005. London: Sage.

59. ONS (2011) Office For National Statistics, Key figures for 2001 Census: Census Area Statistics.

60. Ward, Jenni (2008) 'Researching Drug Sellers: An "experiential" account from "the field"', in *Sociological Research Online*, Volume 13, Issue 1.

61. Pahl, Ray (1984) *Divisions of Labour*. Oxford: Blackwell.

62. Rutter & Bryce (2008) 'The Consumption of Counterfeit Goods: "Here Be Pirates?"' in *Sociology*, 42. London: Sage.

63. Pahl, Ray (1984) *Divisions of Labour*. Oxford: Blackwell. See also Harvey, David (2010) *The Enigma of Capital*. Cambridge: Polity.

64. Gay, Peter (ed., 1995) *The Freud Reader*. London: Vintage.

65. Sennett and Cobb (1996 [1972]) *The Hidden Injuries of Class*. London: Faber.

66. Williams, Raymond (2006 [1960]) *Border Country*. Cardigan: Parthian. Williams' autobiographical character in Border Country is undertaking research on population movements in South Wales. He has collected all the data and likens it to ice cubes, neat packets of information. But he is disillusioned with his work and imagines the freezer door, behind which the ice cubes are kept, keeps flinging open, and that this information is not really stable. Lives aren't ice cubes, and nor is experience, it changes from solid to liquid, to gas, and back again, over history, sometimes in one lifetime. The ice cube tray is a container. Williams's metaphor also promotes qualitative over quantitative research, but what the character in Border Country is really after is a change of substance, a change in the culture of community and place. This is what I also chase.

67. Hanson, Steve (2012c) Review of Sal Restivo's 'Red, Black and Objective' by Sal Restivo, in *Sociological Research Online*, May 2012 issue.

68. Guthman, Julie (2008) 'Bringing good food to others: investigating the subjects of alternative food practice' in *Cultural*

Geographies, No.15. London: Sage.

69. Smithers, Rebecca (2009) 'Dig for recovery: allotments boom as thousands go to ground in recession', in The Guardian, Feb 19.

70. Born, B. & Purcell, M. (2006) Avoiding the local trap: scale and food systems in planning research, in *Journal of Planning Education and Research*, Vol.26 No.2. London: Sage.

71. Sonnino, Roberta (2010) Escaping the Local Trap: Insights on Re-localization from School Food Reform, in *Journal of Environmental Policy & Planning*. Vol.12, No.1. London: Routledge.

72. Nietzsche (1991 [1882]) *The Gay Science*. New York: Random House and Thompson, E.P. (1963) *The Making of the English Working Class*. Harmondsworth: Pelican.

73. Warhurst, Pam (2011) Radio 4 You and Yours, IET feature, December 28. London: BBC Radio.

74. Harvey, David (2010) *The Enigma of Capital*. Cambridge: Polity. Pages 215-260.

75. www.incredible-edible-todmorden.co.uk

76. Graff, Vincent (2011) 'Carrots in the car park. Radishes on the roundabout. The deliciously eccentric story of the town growing ALL its own veg', in the Daily Mail, 'Femail' section, December 10.

77. Jones, Owen (2011) *Chavs*. London: Verso.

78. Smith, Darren (1999) 'The Green Potential of West Yorkshire' in *Regional Review* Vol.8, No.2, published by the School of Geography, Leeds University, http://www.geog.leeds.ac.uk/ [accessed 20/02/2012]. See also Smith's (2001) 'Socio-cultural representations of greentrified Pennine rurality' in the Journal of Rural Studies, Vol. 17, No. 4.

79. Graff, Vincent (2011) in the Daily Mail, 'Femail' section, December 10.

80. Barker, Paul (2012) *Hebden Bridge: A Sense of Belonging*.

London: Frances Lincoln. See also Heywood, Heywood and Jennings (1996) *A History of Todmorden*. Otley: Smith Settle. Law, Brian (1995) *The Fieldens of Todmorden – A Nineteenth Century Business Dynasty*. Littleborough: Kelsall.

81. Sonnino, Roberta (2010) Escaping the Local Trap: Insights on Re-localization from School Food Reform, in *Journal of Environmental Policy & Planning*. Vol.12, No.1. London: Routledge. Also Sonnino (2011) Radio 4 You and Yours, IET feature, December 28. London: BBC Radio.

82. Guthman, Julie (2008) 'Bringing good food to others: investigating the subjects of alternative food practice' in *Cultural Geographies*, No.15. London: Sage. Page 433.

83. Edwards, Jeanette (1998) 'The Need for a "Bit of History": Place and Past in English Identity' in Lovell, N. (ed.) *Locality and Belonging*. London: Routledge.

84. Guthman, Julie (2008) op cit, page 433.

85. Guthman, Julie (2008) op cit.

86. Graff, Vincent (2011) in the Daily Mail, 'Femail' section, December 10.

87. Todmorden News, August 25, 2011.

88. Marx & Engels (1975 [1848]) *Manifesto of the Communist Party*. People's Republic of China Edition, Foreign Languages Press, Peking.

89. Graff, Vincent (2011) op cit.

90. Guthman, Julie (2008) 'Bringing good food to others: investigating the subjects of alternative food practice' in *Cultural Geographies*, No.15. London: Sage, page 437.

91. Skeggs, Beverley (1997) *Formations of Class and Gender*. London: Sage.

92. Savage, et al (2010) 'Dis-identification and class identity' in Silva and Warde, et al, *Cultural analysis and Bourdieu's legacy: settling accounts and developing alternatives. Culture, Economy and the Social*. London: Routledge.

93. Hanson, Steve (2009a) 'Occupation Health' in *Social*

Alternatives, Vol.28, No.1. Australia: University of the Sunshine Coast.

94. Benjamin, Walter (1999 [1940]) 'Theses on the Philosophy of History' and 'The Task of the Translator', in *Illuminations*. London: Pimlico.

95. Graham Crow described Rosser and Harris's 1965 'The Family and Social Change' in (2000) 'Developing Sociological Arguments Through Community Studies', in *International Journal of Social Research Methodology*, Vol.3, No.3. London: Routledge.

96. Crow, Graham (2002) 'Community Studies: Fifty Years of Theorization', in *Sociological Research Online*, Vol.7, No.3, http://www.socresonline.org.uk/7/3/crow.html [accessed 28/06/10].
See also Crow, Graham, (2008) 'Recent rural community studies', in the *International Journal of Research Methodology*, Vol.11, No.2. London: Routledge.

97. Frankenberg, Ronald (1989 [1957]) *Village on the Border*. Waveland Press Incorporated.

98. Bauman (1998) 'On Glocalization: Or Globalisation for some, Localisation for Others', in *Thesis Eleven*, No.54. London: Sage.

99. Bourdieu (1993) *Sociology in Question*. London: Sage.

100. Benjamin, Walter (1999 [1940]) 'Theses on the Philosophy of History' and 'The Task of the Translator', in *Illuminations*. London: Pimlico. Page 247.

101. Deleuze & Guattari (1983) *Anti-Oedipus, Capitalism and Schizophrenia*. London: Continuum, and (1988) *A Thousand Plateaus*. New York: Athlone.

102. Crow, Graham (2002) 'Community Studies: Fifty Years of Theorization', in *Sociological Research Online*, Vol.7, No.3, http://www.socresonline.org.uk/7/3/crow.html [accessed 28/06/10].

103. Hanson and Rainey (2013) 'The Urbis Building as Looking

Glass', in *Cultural Studies*, forthcoming. London: Routledge; goo.gl/of4iv

104. Ravetz, Amanda (2001) *Vision, Knowledge and the Invention of Place in an English Town*. Unpublished PhD thesis, University of Manchester, John Rylands library.

Contemporary culture has eliminated both the concept of the public and the figure of the intellectual. Former public spaces – both physical and cultural – are now either derelict or colonized by advertising. A cretinous anti-intellectualism presides, cheerled by expensively educated hacks in the pay of multinational corporations who reassure their bored readers that there is no need to rouse themselves from their interpassive stupor. The informal censorship internalized and propagated by the cultural workers of late capitalism generates a banal conformity that the propaganda chiefs of Stalinism could only ever have dreamt of imposing. Zer0 Books knows that another kind of discourse – intellectual without being academic, popular without being populist – is not only possible: it is already flourishing, in the regions beyond the striplit malls of so-called mass media and the neurotically bureaucratic halls of the academy. Zer0 is committed to the idea of publishing as a making public of the intellectual. It is convinced that in the unthinking, blandly consensual culture in which we live, critical and engaged theoretical reflection is more important than ever before.